Unit 1-What is She Like?

Get Started

Part A

1. Ask Ss a short warm-up question such as...

    -What do you look like?

    -How tall are you?

2. Have Ss look at the pictures.

3. As a class, elicit descriptions of each of the people in the picture.

    -What does Amanda look like?

    -What does Tony look like?

    -What does Lisa look like?

    -What does Scott look like?

4. Make sure the elicited descriptions include height, build, and hair color words such as...

    tall, short, medium/average height, fat, skinny, medium weight/build, brown hair-brunette, blonde hair, white, black

5. Have Ss, in pairs, fill in each person's height, build, and hair color.

6. Ask one pair to describe one person. Tell them they should speak in complete sentences instead of just reading their lists.

7. Have Ss, in pairs, ask and answer questions 1-4.

8. Elicit the answers to questions 1-4.

9. Ask some follow-up questions such as...

    -Who is in the worst shape?

    -Who is the tallest?

    -Who is the shortest?

    -Who looks the oldest?

    -Who looks the youngest?

    -Who is pretty?

    -Who is unattractive?

10. Ask a short discussion question such as...

    -Which person do you want to look like?

    -What is Amanda/Tony/Lisa/Scott's best feature?

    -What is Amanda/Tony/Lisa/Scott's worst feature?

Part B

1. Ask a short warm-up question such as...

    -What is your personality like?

    -What is your best friend's personality like?

2. Have Ss, individually, match the words with the correct descriptions.

3. Elicit the correct answers by asking questions such as...

    -What is Sarah like?

    -Who is outgoing?

    -What is Jamie like?

    -Who is narrow-minded?

    -What is Jody like?

    -Who is selfish?

4. Have Ss, in small groups, decide which personality words are positive and negative and discuss why.

5. Ask for volunteers to tell the class what their group discussed.

6. Choose 2 Ss to read the example below in front of the class.

7. Have Ss, in pairs, ask and answer similar questions to the example.

8. Ask Ss to give other examples of each personality word.

9. Ask Ss a short discussion question such as...

    -Who is outgoing? Give me an example of how you are outgoing.

    -Who is reliable? Give me an example.

    -Who is adventurous? Give me an example.

    -Is anyone selfish? conservative? narrow-minded?

Talk Together

1. Ask a short warm-up question such as...

    -What are the people in the picture doing?

    -What are they talking about?

2. Have Ss listen to the dialogue once with their books open.

3. Ask Ss some yes or no questions such as...

    -Is Nick single?

    -Does Jasmine's friend have curly hair?

    -Will Nick and Jasmine's friend go on a blind date?

4. Have Ss, in pairs, read the dialogue together, taking turns being Nick and Jasmine.

5. Have Ss listen to the dialogue one more time with their books closed.

6. Check Ss' understanding by asking questions such as...

    -What is Jasmine's friend's job?

    -How old is she?

    -What does she look like?

    -What is her personality?

7. Ask Ss a short discussion question such as...

    -Has this situation ever happened to you?

    -Who has been on a blind date?

    -Do you think blind dates are a good way to meet new people? Why?

Language Focus

1. Have Ss look at the example box.

2. Explain to Ss the two questions and the many different ways to answer.

3. Have Ss, individually, read the question and answers.

4. Elicit more specific questions from Ss, and write them on the board.

    -How do you ask about someone's age?

    -How do you ask about someone's height?

    -How do you ask about someone's build?

    -How do you ask about someone's hair?

    -Is there another way to ask about someone's personality?

5. Have Ss, in pairs, ask each other the questions and choose one of the example answers given.
6. Write some people on the board such as...your mother, your best friend, your boss/senior
7. Have Ss ask each other about those people using some of the questions and answer forms given.
8. Ask Ss a short discussion question such as...
    -What do you like your girlfriend/boyfriend to look like?
    -What personality do you like in a girlfriend/boyfriend?
    -How do you like to be described?

Practice More
Part A

1. Have Ss look at the four pictures and ask a short warm-up question such as...
    -Who do you think is good-looking?
2. Elicit descriptions of each person in the picture, based on the Langauge Focus on the previous page.
    -What does Eric look like?
    -What does Ann look like?
    -What does Robert look like?
    -What does Heather look like?
3. Have Ss, individually, match the descriptions at the bottom to the pictures.
4. Have Ss, in pairs, ask each other about the people in the pictures. Tell Ss they should give a full description, using the examples from the previous page and the descriptions given.
5. Tell them to use the example given.

6. Check Ss' understanding by asking some Ss...

    -Who is muscular?

    -Who has a mustache?

    -Who has freckles on his/her cheeks?

    -Who has wrinkles around his/her eyes?

    -Who wears his/her hair in a ponytail?

    -Who wears his/her hair in braids?

7. Ask Ss a short discussion question such as...

    -Does anyone in class have freckles?

    -Does anyone in class wear his/her hair in braids or a ponytail?

    -Does anyone in class wear glasses?

Part B

1. Ask Ss a short warm-up question such as...

    -What do you think Heather's personality is like?

    -Why do you think so?

2. Have Ss look at the personality words given.

3. Elicit a description of the words that weren't previously used...

    -What does it mean to be shy?

    -What does it mean to be cheerful?

    -What does it mean to be generous?

    -What does it mean to be flexible.

4. Have Ss, individually, choose a person from the pictures above (other than Heather) and write down what they think their personality is like in the box given.

5. Have Ss, in small groups, describe the person they chose using the words given and why they think that person is like that.

6. Ask Ss about the people...

    -Who chose Eric?

    -What is Eric's personality? Why do you think so?

    -Who chose Ann?

    -What is Ann's personality? Why do you think so?

    -Who chose Robert?

    -What is Robert's personality? Why do you think so?

7. Have Ss, individually, choose 2 other people from their life and pick words to describe their personality. They should write them in the box.

8. Have Ss, in pairs, ask about each other's people. Tell them to use the example given.

9. Have Ss change pairs and ask again.

10. Ask some Ss to share their descriptions with the class.

11. Ask Ss a short discussion question such as...

    -Who here is talkative? Give an example.

    -Who here is hardworking? Give an example.

    -Who here is flexible? Give an example.

Let's do it! 1

Part A

1. Ask Ss a warm-up question such as...

    -Where do you think these people are?

    -What does the woman with the hat look like?

    -What does the boy with the soccer ball look like?

2. Have Ss listen to the conversation between Austin and Sarah. Tell them to label each person with his/her name.

3. Have Ss, in pairs, compare their answers.

4. Ask Ss some yes or no questions such as...

    -Is Tyler wearing sunglasses?

    -Is Nicole wearing pink shorts?

    -Does Kevin look like he's in his mid-40s?

    -Is the girl in the orange dress Nicole?

    -Is Nick overweight?

5. Ask a short discussion question such as...

    -Do you have a high school yearbook?

    -Do you keep in touch with people from high school?

    -Do you remember all the people you went to high school with?

Part B

1. Have Ss listen to the conversation again and fill in the description of each person as much as they can.
2. Have Ss listen to the conversation one more time and finish filling in the blanks.
3. Elicit the appearance of each person.

    -What does Tyler look like?

    -What does Nicole look like?

    -What does Nick look like?

    -What does Melissa look like?

    -What does Kevin look like?

4. Have Ss listen one more time and tell them to write down other information given about the classmates
5. Check Ss' understanding by asking questions such as...

    -Who was the top student in Austin's class?

    -Can Sarah easily remember people she went to high school with?

    -Can Austin easily remember people he went to high school with? Why?

    -Who loved playing sports and was well-built?

    -Who did Austin date in high school?

    -Who else was a couple in high school?

    -Who was student body president in grade 12?

6. Ask a short discussion question such as...

    -Who liked to play sports in high school?

    -Did you have a student body president in high school? Do you remember him/her?

    -Were there a lot of couples at your high school?

Part C

1. Choose one student to read the example description to the class.
2. Check Ss' understanding by asking some questions such as...

    -How old is this person?

    -What is her hair like?

    -What is her job?

3. Have Ss write a short description, similar to the example, of someone they know. Tell them to be specific.
4. Have Ss, in pairs, read their descriptions to each other, while their partner draws a picture of the person.
5. Have the pairs compare the picture and the description.
6. Ask for volunteers to share their description and their partner's drawing.
7. Have Ss choose the drawing that most closely matches the description.
8. Ask Ss a short discussion question such as...

    -Which movie star do you think is really beautiful or handsome?

    -What does he/she look like?

    -Are Hollywood movie stars are better looking than the movie stars here? Why?

Let's do it! 2

Part A

1. Ask Ss a short warm-up question such as...

    -What kind of personality do you look for in a friend?

2. Have Ss look at the four different personality descriptions given.
3. Have Ss, individually, write at least one name of someone they know under each description.

4. Have Ss, individually, write one name of a famous or well-known person in their country who is similar to the descriptions.
5. Have Ss, in small groups, discuss the people they wrote down.
6. Ask Ss to share some of the famous people they chose.
7. Ask Ss how many agree/disagree with their classmates and have a small debate.

Part B
1. Have Ss listen to the descriptions and fill in the chart as much as they can.
2. Have Ss listen again and finish filling in the chart.
3. Ask Ss some yes or no questions such as...

    -Is Andy a funny guy?

    -Does Professor Anderson allow students to hand in their papers late?

    -Is the mom a good listener?

    -Is Ray lazy?

4. Have Ss listen to the descriptions one by one and ask the following questions after each one.

    Description 1

    -Which words describe Professor Anderson?

    -How is Professor Anderson strict?

    -Why do his classes always fill up quickly?

    Description 2

    -Which words describe Ray?

    -How is Ray intelligent?

    -Is Ray hard-working?

    -What does Ray want to do in the future?

    Description 3

    -Which words describe Andy?

    -How is Andy humorous?

    -What is Andy known as?

Description 4

-Which words describe this mom?

-How is she warm-hearted?

-What does this mom do for her child?

5. Ask Ss a short discussion question such as...

   -Which of these people do you admire?

   -Which of these people would you like to be friends with?

   -Which of these people are most similar to you?

Part C

1. Have Ss look that the three descriptions below the table.
2. Choose one student to read each description and the reason why.
3. Have Ss choose 3 people that they chose in Part A, or other people in their lives.
4. Have Ss write down the name of the person, their personality, and the reason he/she is like that.
5. Tell Ss to think of an example to support their personality.
6. Have Ss, in pairs, tell each other about the people they chose.
7. Have Ss change pairs and tell other people about the people they chose.
8. Have each student present one of their descriptions in front of the class. Encourage classmates to ask questions if they are not specific enough.
9. Ask Ss a short discussion question such as...

   -What kind of personality is bad?

   -Do you know anyone that has a bad personality?

   -What is the worst personality adjective?

Reading

Part A

1. Ask Ss a warm-up question such as...

    -Do you look at bulletin boards?

    -Do you look at online job advertisements?

2. Have Ss, in groups of 3, read the 3 job advertisements listed. Each person should read one.

3. Check Ss' understanding by asking questions such as...

    -What play will the actor/actress be in?

    -What kind of tutor does Julia want?

    -What kind of person is Katy looking for?

4. Have Ss, in pairs, discuss whether they could be the right person for the want ads given.

5. Ask a few Ss to explain why they could or couldn't be the right person for each of the ads.

Part B

1. Have Ss, in pairs, ask and answer the four questions listed.

2. Ask the class the following questions...

    -Is the actor/actress ad a good opportunity? Would you do it?

    -Is the private tutor ad a good opportunity? Would you do it?

    -Is the campus model a good opportunity? Would you do it?

3. After each question, put the Ss into two groups, those who answered yes and those who answered no.

4. Have the yes group and the no group discuss their reason for their answer.

5. Have the two groups debate why it is a good opportunity or a bad opportunity.

6. Ask Ss a short discussion question such as...

    -What kind of personality makes a good leader/boss?

    -What kind of personality makes a good employee?

    -What kind of personality makes a good friend?

Writing

Part A

1. Ask Ss a warm-up question such as...

    -Are you good at remembering people?

2. Have Ss, in pairs, answer 1-4. Tell them to try to think of as many descriptive words as possible.
3. Have Ss, individually, read the brainstorming example and the writing example.
4. Choose one student to read the writing example to the class.
5. Have Ss choose one person to write about. Tell them they should include as many details as possible.
6. Have Ss, in class or at home, do a similar brainstorming activity.
7. Have Ss, in class or at home, use their brainstormed ideas to write a descriptive paragraph.
8. Have a few Ss present their passage to the class.

Unit 2- What did you use to do when you were younger?

Get Started

Part A

1. Have Ss look at the pictures of the three people and ask a warm-up question such as...

    -What do you think these people do?

2. Have Ss, in groups of 3, read the three histories. Each student should read one.

3. Check Ss' understanding by asking yes or no questions such as...

    -Did Sam study history in university?

    -Did Lucy always like musicals?

    -Is Steve from San Diego?

4. Have Ss, in pairs, ask and answer questions 1-3.

5. Elicit the correct answers to questions 1 and 2.

6. Have Ss walk around and tell their short personal histories to at least 2 other classmates.

7. Ask a few Ss to volunteer to tell the class their personal history.

8. Ask a short discussion question such as...

    -Which of these people has the most interesting history?

    -Why?

    -Which of these people has the most normal history?

    -Why?

Part B

1. Ask a warm-up question such as...

    -What did you like to do last year?

2. As a class, go through each of the activities listed and decide if they are things you do as a kid, as a teen, as a university student, or now. For example:

    When do people play with dolls?

    When do people hang out with friends? etc.

3. Have Ss, individually, write the activities they used to like in the correct time period.
4. Have Ss, in pairs, compare their answers and write down at least 2 or 3 other things they liked to do at those time periods.
5. Elicit other activities for each time period.
6. Ask Ss a short discussion question such as...

    -How have your activities changed from your childhood?

    -How have your activities changed from your university years?

    -Why do you think they've changed?

Talk Together

1. Ask Ss a warm-up question such as...

    -What do you think the person in the picture likes to do?

2. Have Ss listen to the dialogue once with their books open.
3. Ask Ss some yes or no questions such as...

    -Was George born in Texas?

    -Does Lucy like CDs?

    -Does George still play the electric guitar today?

4. Have Ss, in pairs, read the dialogue, taking turns being Lucy and George.
5. Have Ss listen to the dialogue one more time with books closed.
6. Check Ss' understanding by asking questions such as...

    -What kind of music did George like in high school?

    -How many CDs does Lucy have?

    -Where did George go to college?

    -Where does George play the electric guitar now?

7. Ask Ss a short discussion question such as...

    -What did you like to do in high school?

    -Has your music choice changed since high school?

    -Do you play a musical instrument?

Language Focus

1. Have Ss, in pairs, ask each other the questions and answer with the one given.
2. Have Ss, in different pairs, ask each other the questions and answer for themselves.
3. Have Ss stand up and walk around the room and find someone that shares the same answer as them.

    For example:

    This is Joe, he and I studied English in university.

    Have the pair present their shared answer to the class.
4. Ask Ss a short discussion question such as...

    -Are most of your friends the same age as you?

    -Was anyone born in this city?

    -How many people used to study English as a kid?

Practice More

Part A

1. Ask Ss a warm-up question such as...

    -Is the past important for the future?
2. Have Ss, individually, write down their personal history, using the questions and answers given. Tell Ss they must write in complete sentences.
3. Have Ss, in pairs, ask each other the questions. Tell them they may want to write down their partner's answers.
4. Have Ss present their partner to the class. Make sure they use complete sentences.
5. Ask Ss a short discussion question such as...

    -Did your favorite subject change from elementary school to high school?

    -Do you visit your birthplace often?

    -What is your earliest memory?

Part B

1. Ask Ss a warm-up question such as...

    -Were your teenage days hard for you?

2. Choose two Ss to demonstrate how to ask and answer the questions given, using the samples.

3. Have Ss, in pairs, ask and answer the questions for themselves.

4. Have Ss change pairs and ask and answer the questions again.

5. Take a poll of the class to see what the most popular future job was for the class. Ask Ss why that was the most popular.

6. Ask Ss a short discussion question such as...

    -Were you nice to your parents as a teenager?

    -Did you like studying when you were a teenager?

    -Did you spend a lot of time with friends when you were a teenager?

Part C

1. Ask Ss a warm-up question such as...

    -Was turning 20 a great birthday for you? Why or why not?

2. Choose two Ss to demonstrate how to ask and answer the questions given, using the samples.

3. Have Ss, in pairs, ask and answer the questions for themselves.

4. Have Ss change pairs and ask and answer the questions again.

5. Take a poll of the class to see what the most popular free time activities were at 20 years old. Ask Ss why that was the most popular.

6. Ask Ss a short discussion question such as...

    -How does life change after 20?

    -Do you have more freedom after 20?

    -Were your university and high school years very different?

Let's do it! 1

Part A

1. Ask Ss a warm-up question such as...

    -Do you think most people of your age enjoyed doing the same things as a kid?

    -Do you think most people of your age enjoyed doing the same things as a teenager?

    -Do you think most people of your age doing the same things as a university student?

2. Have Ss, individually, look at all the activities listed and circle the ones they have done in their life.

3. Have Ss, individually write those activities into the spider web according to when they used to do them.

4. Have Ss, in pairs, compare each other's spider webs.

5. Have the pairs note the activities that they have in common during the same time period.

6. Have each pair tell their common activities to the class. Give the following demonstration if necessary...

    We both got good grades when we were kids and teenagers. We both played a lot of sports as teenagers etc.

7. Ask Ss a short discussion question such as...

    -Are there any activities that you NEVER did?

    -Are some of these activities more male? more female? Why?

    -Which of these activities are positive?

    -Are any of these activities negative?

Part B

1. Have Ss listen to the three conversations all at once and fill in the numbers beside the activities as much as they can.

2. Check Ss' answers by asking questions such as...

    -Which conversation talked about reading comic books?

    -Which conversation talked about going to the orchestra?

    -Which conversation talked about going scuba diving?

    -Which conversation talked about playing the violin?

3. Have Ss listen to the conversations one by one and finish filling in the numbers.

4. Ask the following questions after each conversation.

    Conversation 1

    -What activities were in this conversation?

    -When did person B play with pets?

    -Why did person A like scuba diving?

    -What happened when person B played games?

    Conversation 2

    -What activities were in this conversation?

    -What did the wild person do as a teenager?

    -What did the laid-back person do as a teenager?

    -Where did person B go camping?

    Conversation 3

    -What activities were in this conversation?

    -Why did person B like the Philharmonic Orchestra?

    -How many comic books did person A read?

    -Why did person A not become a comic book writer?

5. Have Ss check the activities that they like to do or previously liked to do.

6. Ask Ss a short discussion question such as...

    -Who liked to listen to jazz when they were younger?

    -Who has been scuba diving?

    -Who used to have pets?

Part C

1. Choose two Ss to demonstrate the example dialogue.
2. Have Ss, in pairs, talk about what they liked to do as a kid, as a teenager, and as a university student.
3. Tell Ss to use the activities in Part A and B and any other activities they want.
4. Have Ss change pairs and talk about it again.
5. Ask for a few volunteers to talk about their past likes in front of the class.
6. Ask Ss a short discussion question such as...

    -What do you think kids like to do nowadays?

    -What do you think teenagers like to do nowadays?

    -What do you think university students like to do nowadays?

Let's do it! 2

Part A

1. Ask Ss a warm-up question such as...

    -Do you have a blog?

    -What are some good things about having a blog?
2. Have Ss, individually, complete the chart using complete sentences.
3. Have Ss, in pairs, share their history with each other.
4. Ask a few Ss some of the questions...

    -What do you like to do now?

    -What did you like to do as a kid?

    -Where were you born?

    -When were you born?

Part B

1. Ask Ss a warm-up question such as...

    -Do you ever watch talk shows?
2. Have Ss listen to the three clips and mark the sentences as true and false as much as they can.

3. Check Ss' answers by asking some questions such as...

    -Did Kimberly start writing short stories when she was 15?

    -Did Tim major in construction?

    -Did Nick decide to become a chef when he was in France?

4. Have Ss listen to the clips one by one and finish marking true and false.

5. After each clip, ask the following questions...

    Clip 1

    -What is Kimberly Johnson's job?

    -Was "The Hero" Kimberly's first published novel?

    -What is Kimberly's advice to young people dreaming of becoming a writer?

    Clip 2

    -Where does Nick work?

    -Why did Nick want to go to France?

    -What is Nick's advice to the young audience?

    Clip 3

    -What is Tim Oliver's job?

    -How did Tim start in fashion design?

    -Who loves Tim?

6. Ask Ss a short discussion question such as...

    -Which story do you like best? Why?

    -How important do you think a university major is? Why?

    -Is it important to never give up?

    -Is it bad to start from the bottom?

Part C

1. Have Ss, in pairs, pretend to be a TV talk show host and a guest.
2. Have them take turns interviewing each other and using their personal histories and the listening script as an example.
3. Choose one pair of Ss to present their talk show interview to the class.
4. Have Ss think of a dream job and how to get it.

5. Have Ss, in different pairs, interview each other with their dream jobs and pretend histories.

6. Choose a few pairs to present their made-up talk show interview to the class.

7. Ask Ss a short discussion question such as...

    -Do you know a lot of history about your friends?

    -Do you know a lot of history about your parents?

    -Do you know a lot of history about famous people?

Reading

1. Ask Ss a warm-up question such as...

    -Do you know how your parents met?

2. Have Ss, in pairs, read the two stories. Each student should read one story.

3. Choose two volunteers to read the stories in front of the class.

4. Check Ss' understanding by asking questions such as...

    -What is the girl's nationality?

    -How long did her parents save money?

    -Does she have any brothers or sisters?

    -Who is Steven Paul Jobs?

    -What did he do?

    -When was he born?

    -Did he graduate from college?

5. Ask Ss a short discussion question such as...

    -How do these stories make you feel?

    -What is the first story's message?

    -What is the second story's message?

Part B

1. Have Ss, in small groups, answer questions 1-3

2. As a class, ask questions 1 and 2.

3. Ask for volunteers to discuss any turning points in their lives.

4. Ask Ss a short discussion question such as...

   -Do you like to read inspiring stories?

   -Do you ever read biographies?

   -Who is a famous person from your country with a good history?

Writing

Part A

1. Have Ss look at the two situations and choose the one that's appropriate for their age.
2. Have them write the answers to the questions.
3. Have Ss, in pairs, discuss their past using the questions and answers given.

Part B

1. Choose one student to read the example in front of the class.
2. Have Ss, in class or at home, write a similar passage based on some of the questions in Part A.
3. Have some Ss read their passage.

Unit 3- What do you do to stay in shape?

Get Started

Part A

1. Ask Ss a warm-up question such as...

    -What does it mean to stay in shape?

    -Do you think it's important to stay in shape?

2. Have Ss look at the four pictures and elicit a description of each.

    -What's happening in this picture?

3. Have Ss, individually, check the activities on the list they do to stay in shape.

4. Go through each activity and take a poll of how many Ss do each activity.

    -How many of you exercise regularly? etc.

5. Go through the activities again and ask about the importance.

    -How many of you think you should exercise regularly?

6. Have Ss, in small groups, decide which healthy habit is the most important.

7. Have each group explain why they think that habit is most important.

    -Example: We think taking vitamins is the most important healthy habit because your body needs vitamins. Also, vitamins give you lots of energy.

8. Have Ss, in the same groups, decide which healthy habit is least important.

9. Have each group explain why they think that habit is least important.

    -Example: We think that sleeping more than six hours a night is the least important habit because your body doesn't need that much sleep. Five to six hours is plenty of sleep during the week. Then the weekend is a good time to get some extra sleep.

10. Have Ss debate their answers with each other.

11. Ask Ss a short discussion question such as...

    -Which healthy habit is most important for young people? Why?

    -Which healthy habit is most important for older people? Why?

    -Are there any healthy habits that are more important for women?

    -Are there any healthy habits that are more important for men?

Part B

1. Have Ss, in pairs, match the verbs to the healthy activities to make expressions.
2. Give the following demonstration if necessary...

    -Can you say do in shape? No

    -Can you say be in shape? Yes
3. Tell Ss many of the verbs up top can be used with more than one of the phrases at the bottom.
4. Ask each student to make a phrasal verb using the expressions they wrote down.
5. Have Ss, in pairs, write down one sentence and one question using the combinations they made.
6. Have Ss stand up and walk around and ask each other questions and tell each other sentences using the expressions.
7. Ask Ss a short discussion question, using the expressions, such as...

    -How often do you get exercise?

    -How many people want to get in shape?

    -Is anyone on a diet? What kind of diet?

Talk Together

Part A

1. Have Ss look at the picture and ask a warm-up question such as...

    -Which person is in better shape?

    -What do you think they are talking about?
2. Have Ss listen to the dialogue once with books open.
3. Check Ss' understanding by asking some yes or no questions such as...

    -Does Kate run in the park?

    -Is Jason in shape?

    -Does Kate eat a lot of fatty foods for dinner?
4. Have Ss, in pairs, read the dialogue, taking turns being Kate and Jason.
5. Have Ss listen one more time with books closed.

6. Elicit the correct answers to some of the following questions...

   -How much exercise does Kate get?

   -What is Kate wearing?

   -What does Kate eat for dinner?

   -How does Jason feel about his body?

7. Ask Ss a short discussion question such as...

   -What is a fad diet?

   -Have you ever tried a fad diet?

   -How much exercise do you think a person should get every week?

Language Focus

1. Ask Ss a warm-up question such as...

   -In the previous section, how often did Kate go jogging?

2. Have Ss, individually, read over the Frequency Expressions.

3. Ask some Ss, "How often do you go jogging?"

4. Have each student write down two other forms of exercise. Tell them to try and be creative.

5. Have Ss, in pairs, ask each other the frequency expressions. Tell Ss to first ask their partner about jogging, then ask their partner about the other forms of exercise they wrote down.

6. Ask Ss to volunteer to tell what their form of exercise is and how often they do it.

7. Have Ss, individually, read over the verb+to-infinitive section.

8. Ask some Ss the questions in the verb+to-infinitive section, tell them to answer for themselves.

9. Ask Ss a similar question to that in the verb+to-infinitive section...

   -What can you do to lose weight?

   -What do your friends advise you to do to be healthy?

   -What does your mother advise you to do to be healthy?

10. Have Ss, individually, look at the verb+gerund section.

11. Ask Ss the questions given in the verb+gerund section. Tell them to answer for themselves.

12. Ask Ss some other questions similar to the ones in verb+gerund section...

    -How much time do you spend exercising in a week?

    -Do you spend a lot of time walking around the city?

13. Ask Ss a short discussion question such as...

    -How much time do you spend swimming in the summer?

    -What do you do to relieve stress?

    -How much time do you spend exercising at the gym?

Extra: Have Ss take their other forms of exercise that they wrote down previously and make a sentence using verb+to-infinitive and a sentence using verb+gerund.

Practice More

Part A

1. Ask Ss a warm-up questions such as...

    -Do you think you're a healthy person?

2. Have Ss, individually, check yes or no for themselves for the lifestyle and habits listed.

3. Have Ss, in partners, ask each other the yes or no questions.

4. Take a poll of the class by asking some of the yes or no questions and writing down how many people say yes.

5. Ask Ss a short discussion question, using the information taken from the poll, such as...

    -Why do you think most people do this?

    -Why do you think most people don't do this?

    -What is the best thing on the lifestyle and habit list?

    -What is the worst thing on the lifestyle and habit list?

Part B

1. Have Ss, in pairs, read the example given.
2. Have Ss, in pairs, ask their partner how often he/she does the activities listed above.
3. Tell Ss to write their partners answers down in the chart.
4. Ask a few Ss to tell you how often their partner does something, such as...

    -How often does your partner drink coffee? How often do you drink coffee?

    -How often does your partner eat fruits and vegetables? How often do you?

    -How often does your partner go to bed early? How often do you?

5. Ask Ss a short discussion question such as...

    -Which lifestyle and habits listed above are positive?

    -Which lifestyle and habits listed above are negative?

    -How often should you go to bed early?

    -How often should you smoke?

    -How often should you go for regular medical check-ups?

Part C

1. Have Ss, individually, write down some other lifestyle or habits similar to the ones in the chart.
2. Tell Ss they should write down two negative habits and two positive habits.
3. Have Ss, in pairs, ask their partners about the habits they wrote down...Give the following example if necessary...

    -Do you eat late at night?

    -How often do you eat late at night?

    -Do you play sports?

    -How often do you play sports?

4. Have Ss, in pairs, ask each other the question in the example, "What do you do to stay healthy?" "What do you do to stay in shape?"

5. Tell Ss they should include all the activities in the chart and the ones they and their partner came up with in their answer. Give the following example if necessary...

   -What do you do to stay healthy?

   -I exercise three times a week. I eat a lot of fruits and vegetables everyday. I go to bed early probably about four times a week. I don't smoke. etc.

6. Ask for volunteers to share with the class how they stay in shape or stay healthy.

7. Ask a short discussion question such as...

   -How often do you participate in unhealthy activities?

   -Are your friends pretty healthy?

   -Is your family pretty healthy?

   -Do you think young people are healthier than older people?

Let's do it! 1

Part A

1. Ask Ss a warm-up question such as...

   -Do you think you are in excellent, good, or average shape?

2. Have Ss, in pairs, give each other the fitness quiz given below.

3. Tell them to take turns answering the questions given and they should calculate their partner's score.

4. Ask Ss a short discussion question such as...

   -Do you believe this quiz?

   -Why do you/don't you trust this quiz?

   -Do you ever do online or magazine quizzes similar to this one?

Part B

1. Write the following questions on the board...

   Is being healthy important to you?--Why or Why not?

   What do you do that's bad for you?

   What can you do to improve your health?

2. Have Ss walk around the room and talk about their health with at least four different Ss.
3. Tell them to use the example given in the book and the three questions on the board.
4. Ask a few Ss to share some things about their discussions with the class.
5. Ask a short discussion question such as...

    -What do you think is the biggest health problem is in this country?

    -What do you think is not a health problem for this country?

    -What is the easiest health problem to solve?

Part C

1. Have Ss look at the four pictures. Ask them a warm-up question such as...

    -Which person is healthy?

    -Which person is unhealthy?

2. Have Ss listen to the conversation between John and Tracy and complete the sentences as best they can.
3. Ask Ss some yes or no questions such as...

    -Is Tracy in good shape?

    -Does John exercise a lot?

    -Does John eat better than Tracy?

4. Have Ss listen to the conversation one more time and finish filling in the blanks.
5. Check Ss' understanding by asking questions such as...

    -How does John describe Tracy?

    -How often does Tracy go jogging?

    -How often does John exercise?

    -What does John enjoy eating?

    -What is Tracy's advice to John?

6. Have Ss, in pairs, discuss how healthy Tracy and John are.
7. Have Ss, in pairs, decide what advice, if any they would give to both Tracy and John.
8. Ask a few pairs to share their advice.

9. Ask Ss a short discussion question such as...

    -Are you more like Tracy or John?

    -Can a person exercise too much? How?

    -Can a person diet too much? How?

Let's do it! 2

Part A

1. Ask Ss a warm-up question such as...

    -Do you think most women are healthier than men? Why or Why not?

2. Have Ss look at the pictures and elicit a description...

    -What is Jesse doing in the picture?

    -What is Laura doing in the picture?

3. Have Ss listen to Jesse and Laura's descriptions and fill in the chart as much as they can.

4. Have Ss listen to both of them again.

5. Ask Ss some yes or no questions such as...

    -Does Jesse's family have healthy habits?

    -Is Laura in great shape?

    -Does Jesse eat a lot of fattening foods?

    -Did Laura follow her doctor's advice?

6. Have Ss listen to the descriptions one by one.

7. Check Ss' understanding by asking the following questions after each description...

    Jesse

    -What does Jesse focus on in order to stay healthy?

    -What does Jesse's family like to do together?

    -What does Jesse have everyday?

    Laura

    -What was Laura's doctor's advice?

    -Why did he give her that advice?

    -What time does Laura usually wake up? What does she do then?

    -Has her diet and exercise plan been successful? How do you know?

8. Have Ss, in pairs, compare their charts and make sure they got the answers correct.
9. Ask Ss some short discussion question such as...

    -Do you think you are more like Laura or Jesse?

    -Do you ever have health problems caused by your lifestyle?

    -How many people play sports or go hiking with their family?

Part B

1. Go over the instructions with Ss and make sure they understand.
2. Have Ss fill in the chart according to how good of shape they are in. Tell them to think about anything they could be doing better and write it in the "No" column.
3. Have Ss, in small groups, compare their answers and their plans to improve.

Part C

1. Have Ss, in new pairs, read the example dialogue, taking turns being part A and B.
2. Have Ss ask each other about how they stay in shape using the answers from Part B.
3. Have Ss switch pairs and do it again.
4. Ask one pair to volunteer and do the dialogue in front of the class.
5. Ask Ss a short discussion question such as...

    -Is this class in pretty good shape?

    -Do you ever give advice to friends and family about their health?

    -Do you know anyone who is in really bad shape?

Reading

Part A

1. Have Ss look at the pictures and ask them a warm-up question such as...

    -What do you think these pictures are trying to say?

    -What do you think this article is about?

2. Have Ss, in small groups, read the health article, taking turns reading the different tips.
3. Choose one student to read the first tip.
4. Ask the following questions...

-What is it telling you to do?

-Do you agree with this tip?

-Do you do this already?

5. Repeat the same questions for each tip.

Part B

1. Have Ss, in small groups, discuss the answers to questions 1-5.
2. As a class, answer the questions together. Try to elicit some different opinions and discuss them as a class.
3. Have Ss look at question 5.
4. Have each student write down 2 health tips other than the ones given in the article. Tell Ss to be creative and think of a reason.
5. Have each student share their tip with the class. Tell the class to agree/disagree with the tips.
6. Ask Ss some short discussion questions such as...

   -What instant food is popular here?

   -How many glasses of water do you drink every day?

   -Do you have a sweet tooth?

Writing

1. Ask Ss a warm-up question such as...

   -Do you and your friends often discuss diet and exercise?

   -Do you and your friends discuss how you look?

2. Have Ss read the example passage.
3. Check Ss' understanding by asking questions such as...

   -What does this person do to stay healthy?

   -How much time do they spend exercising?

   -Do you think this person is healthy? Why or why not?

4. Have Ss write a similar passage about themselves. Tell them to look at the questions at the top for the main subject of their passage. Tell them to be as specific as possible.
5. Have Ss present their passage to the class.

Unit 4- What do you do when you're bored?

Get Started

Part A

1. Ask Ss a warm-up question such as...

    -What do you feel like today?

    -How do you usually feel on Mondays?

    -How do you usually feel on Saturdays?

2. Have Ss, in pairs, look at the pictures and match the feelings with the correct pictures.

3. Elicit the correct feeling by asking...

    -How does the person in this picture feel?

    -How do you know?

4. Have Ss, in small groups, each try and act out a feeling listed, with the other people in their group guessing the feeling.

5. Choose a few Ss to act it out in front of the class. Tell them a specific feeling and let the whole class guess.

6. Ask Ss a short discussion question such as...

    -How often do you feel upset?

    -How often do you feel nervous?

    -How often do you feel tired?

Part B

1. Ask Ss a warm-up question such as...

    -How does English class make you feel? Why?

2. Have Ss, individually, match the situations to the feelings in the chart.

3. Have Ss, in pairs, compare which situations they chose for which feeling.

4. Check Ss' understanding by asking questions such as...(try to elicit more than one feeling from the Ss)

    -How do tricky test questions make you feel? Why?

    -How does making a speech make you feel? Why?

    -How does going on a blind date make you feel? Why?

5. Go through the rest of the situations and ask how they make them feel and why.
6. Have Ss, in pairs, come up with one other situation for each feeling.
7. Have each pair share three situations and explain why they make them feel that way.
8. Ask Ss a short discussion question such as...

    -How does eating a big meal make you feel? Why?

    -How does watching sports on TV make you feel? Why?

    -How does dancing make you feel? Why?

    -How does finishing your homework make you feel? Why?

Talk Together

1. Have Ss look at the picture and elicit a description...

    -What's happening in this picture?

    -How does she look like she feels?

    -How does he look like he feels?

2. Have Ss listen to the dialogue once with books open.
3. Check Ss' understanding by asking yes or no questions such as...

    -Does Janet ever feel depressed?

    -Are Monday mornings fun for them?

    -Does Ben look depressed?

4. Have Ss, in pairs, read the dialogue, taking turns being Ben and Janet.
5. Have Ss listen to the dialogue one more time with books closed.

6. Elicit the correct answers to some of the following questions...

   -Why is Ben depressed?

   -What are the Monday morning blues?

   -What does it mean to have a long face?

   -What does Janet do when she feels depressed?

7. Ask Ss a short discussion question such as...

   -How do you feel on Monday morning?

   -What do you do when you feel depressed?

   -Are you good at hiding your feelings?

Language Focus

1. Ask Ss a warm-up question such as...

   -Why do you feel tired?

2. Have Ss, in pairs, ask and answer the questions given according to the chart.

3. Ask a few Ss one of the questions and elicit the correct answer.

4. Have Ss, individually, write their current feelings and why they feel that way.

5. Have Ss stand up and walk around and ask how their classmates feel, why, and what they do when they feel that way, according to the chart.

6. Ask Ss a short discussion question such as...

   -How often do you truthfully answer the question, "How are you feeling?"?

   -Do you like telling people when you are feeling bad?

   -Do you like telling people when you are feeling good?

Practice More

Part A

1. Have Ss look at the picture of the guy and guess how he is feeling.

2. Have Ss, in pairs, read the example dialogue, taking turns being A and B.

3. Have Ss, in pairs, repeat the dialogue using the feelings and emotions and the reasons given in the chart.

4. Choose one pair of Ss to demonstrate each emotion. Tell them to be creative and really act it out.

5. Have Ss choose two emotions listed and come up with one other reason for the emotions.
6. Have Ss, in pairs, practice asking and explaining their emotions.
7. Choose a few Ss to share their emotions and reasons in front of the class.
8. Ask Ss a short discussion question such as...

    -If someone stole your sandwich off your desk would you be annoyed?

    -Has anyone ever had a surprise party?

    -Do you get scared when you watch horror movies?

Part B

1. Have Ss look at the picture of the woman and guess how she is feeling.
2. Have Ss, in pairs, read the example dialogue, taking turns being A and B.
3. Have Ss, in pairs, repeat the dialogue, using the feelings/emotions, the when and things I do section below.
4. Choose one pair of Ss to demonstrate each emotion. Tell them to be creative and really act it out.
5. Have Ss, in pairs, have a short discussion on the chart. Tell them to discuss whether or not they feel the same way in the When...situation, and whether they do the same things in the Things I do...situation.
6. Have each group share what they discussed.
7. Have Ss, individually, choose one feeling/situation on the chart that they do not experience.
8. Have the Ss change it to fit their experiences. Give the following demonstration if necessary...

    I don't feel afraid when I walk home at night. But I do feel afraid when I am up high on a mountain or a building. When this happens, I try to think positive thoughts and not look down.

9. Have each student share their change with the class.

10. Ask Ss a short discussion question such as...

    -Have you ever fallen down on the street? Did you feel embarrassed?

    -Have you ever had a friend lie to you? How did you handle it?

    -How often do you feel lonely?

Let's do it! 1

Part A

1. Ask Ss a warm-up question such as...

    -When do you feel thrilled?

    -When do you feel guilty?

2. Have Ss look at the words listed in the box to the right.

3. Elicit the meanings of the words from the Ss.

4. Have Ss group the words into positive and negative groups.

5. Have Ss listen to the people talking about how they feel and fill in the feelings next to the person's name.

6. Check Ss' understanding by eliciting the feeling of each person...

    -How does Mike/Claire/Kenneth/Allison/Tom/Gwen feel?

7. Ask Ss a short discussion question such as...

    -Do you often feel frustrated?

    -What are you confident about?

    -Do you feel relieved after you finish a project or test?

Part B

1. Have Ss listen to the people talking about their feelings again and fill in the missing words.

2. Check Ss' understanding by asking some yes or no questions such as...

    -Did Mike fix his problem?

    -Did Allison want to lie to her parents?

    -Did Claire go out with the guy in her photography class?

    -Was Tom too scared to go bungee-jumping?

    -Did Kenneth lose his wallet for good?

    -Has Gwen been having a lot of fun lately?

3. Have Ss listen again, one by one, and finish filling in the blanks.
4. After each person's description, check Ss' understanding by asking questions such as...

    -How does this person feel?

    -Why do they feel that way?

    -Do you understand their feelings? Why or why not?

5. Have Ss, in small groups, discuss if they would feel the same way as the people in the different situations. Tell them they should discuss the following three points...

    -Have you ever been in this situation before?

    -Would you feel the same as this person?

    -Why or why not?

6. Have the groups share with the class the situations that they had disagreements with.

7. Ask Ss a short discussion question such as...

    -Have you ever lied to your parents? Do you think it's wrong?

    -Have you ever lost something? Have you ever turned in something you found?

    -Have you ever done something really dangerous?

Part C

1. Have Ss look at the chart. Tell them to fill in a time they felt that way. If they can't think of a time, tell them they can make one up, as long as its appropriate.
2. Choose 2 Ss to read the example at the bottom of the page.
3. Have Ss, in pairs, talk about their situations together, using the example at the bottom of the page.
4. Present the following situations and ask how it would make a student feel.

    -I spoke English to a native speaker at a party for an hour. He understood me the whole time. Afterwards, I felt very...(confident)

    -I was in a hurry and got caught in traffic. After that I couldn't find a parking space. After I finally parked, I had to walk behind a really big group that was going very slow. I was feeling very...(frustrated)

-I studied for my English exam for months and months. After the exam I didn't really feel like I did a very good job. But when I got the score back, it was excellent. I felt very...(relieved)

-I went traveling in China. There were no English signs at the bus station. I couldn't really read the Chinese. I felt very...(confused)

-I took a taxi home. It was very dark and the taxi driver gave me too much money back. I didn't realize it until I was halfway home. I felt a little...(guilty)

-I've wanted to go to Italy all my life. I have been saving up money for years. I am going next week. I feel really...(thrilled)

5. Ask Ss some short discussion questions such as...

   -Are you an emotional person?

   -Do you often feel confused?

   -What do you do when you feel guilty?

Let's do it! 2

Part A

1. Have Ss look at the four pictures. Ask a warm-up question such as...

   -How do you think he/she feel?

   -How can you tell?

2. Elicit a description of each of the four feelings.

   -What does it mean to feel touched?

   -What does it mean to feel disappointed?

   -What does it mean to feel shocked?

   -What does it mean to feel offended?

3. Have Ss, in pairs, match the feelings and situations to the pictures.

4. Elicit the correct answers by asking...How does Andy/Jasmin/Meg/David feel?

5. Ask Ss a short discussion question such as...

   -How do you feel when someone lies to you?

   -How do you feel when you read a touching story?

   -How do you feel when you hear bad news?

Part B

1. Have Ss listen to the people describing what they do when they feel a certain way and fill in the chart.
2. Elicit the feelings by asking...
   -How did the person in #1 feel? #2? #3? #4?
3. Have Ss listen to the descriptions one by one and finish filling in the chart. Ask the following questions after each.

   1
   -How did this person feel?
   -Why was she scared?
   -What happened with the theif?
   -How does she deal with it now?

   2
   -How did this person feel?
   -Why was he so hurt?
   -How did he solve his problem?
   -What does he do when he thinks of it now?

   3
   -How did this person feel?
   -Why was she so offended?
   -Why should she have gone instead of her male colleague?
   -What does she do to feel better?

   4
   -How did this person feel?
   -Why was she so moved/touched?
   -Where was the diamond ring?
   -What does she do when she thinks about it now?

4. Ask Ss some short discussion questions such as...

   -Have any of these situations ever happened to you?

   -Would you feel the same way?

   -Do you cry during happy times too?

Part C

1. Choose 2 Ss to read the example dialogue in front of the class.
2. Have Ss, in pairs, make up dialogues using the feelings listed and any appropriate situation they can think of. Make sure they mention why they feel that way and what they do to make themselves feel better.
3. Choose a feeling and have one group display their dialogue to the class. Do the same thing for the rest of the feelings listed.
4. Have Ss, in pairs, go through the situations at the bottom of the page and discuss how they would feel about it and how they would deal with it.
5. Tell them they can use the solutions on the right if they need to.
6. Go through each of the situations and get volunteers to explain their answers.
7. Go through each of the solutions, ask Ss, "Who would _____ to feel better?"
8. Ask Ss a short discussion question such as...

   -What do you do when you're angry with a close friend or family member?

   -What do you do when you are really full from eating a big meal?

   -What do you do when you feel really stressed at work or school?

Reading

1. Ask Ss a warm-up question such as...

   -Do you often have embarrassing moments?

   -Do you get embarrassed easily?

2. Have Ss, in groups of 3, read the embarrassing moment articles. Each student should read one passage.
3. Choose one volunteer to read one passage aloud to the class.

4. Check Ss' understanding by asking questions after each passage.

   'Watch out for the boss!'

   -Why did Ken feel embarrassed?

   -What did he say about his boss?

   -What did he do to solve the problem?

   'Faking it!'

   -Why was Scott embarrassed?

   -Who was at the match?

   -What did he do to solve the problem?

   'FALLEN SKIRT'

   -Why was Sonya embarrassed?

   -What were the people around her doing?

   -What did she do to solve the problem?

Part B

1. Have Ss, in pairs, read questions 1-5 and answer them together.
2. Ask the class the first question and encourage someone to tell their story.
3. Choose several Ss to tell their partner's embarrassing story to the class.
4. Have the class vote on which story is the most embarrassing and why.
5. Ask Ss a short discussion question such as...

   -What is the best way to get over an embarrassing situation?

   -Do you and your friends make fun of each other in embarrassing situations?

   -Are you a clumsy person?

Writing

Part A

1. Have Ss, in pairs, briefly answer questions 1-4.
2. Tell Ss to pay attention to the topic that is easiest for them to answer.
3. Ask Ss to share something in their life that makes them happy.

4. Ask Ss some discussion questions by giving them these hypothetical situations...

   -Would you feel very happy if you won the lottery?

   -Would you feel very happy if you drank a beer with a friend tonight?

   -Would you feel very happy if you helped someone in need?

5. Choose one student to read the example in front of the class.

6. Check Ss' understanding by asking questions such as...

   -What are two things that make this person feel happy?

   -Would these things make you feel happy?

   -Do you think that happiness comes from small things or big things?

7. Have Ss, in class or at home, write a short passage on one of the topics listed above. Tell them to be specific and make sure their passage reflects their individuality.

8. Have a few Ss share their passages in class.

Unit 5- Have you ever gone bungee jumping?

Get Started

Part A

1. Ask Ss a warm-up question such as...

    -Do you think you've had a lot of crazy life experiences?

    -Have you ever traveled abroad?

    -Have you ever danced in public?

2. Have Ss, individually, look at the list of things below and check yes or no.

3. Have Ss, in pairs, compare their lists.

4. Have Ss, in pairs, discuss questions 1-4.

5. Ask the class, "Who has _____?" for each thing on the list.

6. Ask the Ss that raise their hands to give some more information about that experience.

    For example...

    -Who has tried Thai food?

    -Did you like it?

    -What was it like?

7. Have Ss, individually, think of two other life experiences they have had and write them at the bottom of the list. If necessary, give an example...

    - I have traveled to Spain.

    -I have driven a car.

    -I have played an instrument in front of other people.

8. Have Ss walk around the room asking their classmates about their experience. Give the following example if necessary...

    -I have traveled to Spain. Have you?

9. Ask a few Ss to say the answers they've found out.

    Maria has ridden a horse.

    Chris has played in a soccer team.

    Amy has been to Tibet.

    Rick has eaten frogs.

Part B

1. Ask Ss a warm-up question such as...

    -Have you been taking classes here for long?

    -Have you known your classmates for long?

    -Have you known your best friend for long?

2. Have Ss, individually, check yes to those activities listed that they have been doing for a long time and write how long they've been doing them.

3. Have Ss, in pairs, ask each other about those activities.

4. As a class, go through the list and ask...

    -Who has been _____ for long?

    -How long have you been _____?

5. Have Ss think of one other question in this form.

6. Have Ss walk around and ask their classmates their questions.

7. Choose a few Ss to share their questions and some of their classmates' answers.

8. Ask Ss a short discussion question such as...

    -How long have you been living in this city?

    -How long have you been living at your current home?

    -How long have you been using a computer?

Talk Together

1. Ask Ss a warm-up question such as...

    -Do you like the snow?

    -Have you ever been skiing?

    -Have you ever been to Japan?

2. Have Ss listen to the dialogue once with books open.

3. Check Ss' understanding by asking some yes or no questions such as...

    -Has Ryan ever visited Japan?

    -Did Marilyn go skiing in Japan?

    -Have they both been to hot springs before?

4. Have Ss, in pairs, read the dialogue, taking turns being Marilyn and Ryan.

5. Have Ss listen to the dialogue once more with books closed.

6. Elicit the correct answers to the following questions...

    -How long was Marilyn in Japan?

    -What did Marilyn do in Japan?

    -What has Ryan done in Japan?

7. Ask Ss a short discussion question such as...

    -Who has taken a business trip abroad?

    -Where? How was it?

    -Who has been to hot springs in Japan?

    -Where? How was it?

Language Focus

1. Have Ss, in pairs, practice asking and answering the questions in the box.
2. Ask some Ss the questions and elicit the answers given.
3. Have Ss, in pairs, ask each other the questions and answer for themselves.
4. Ask some Ss the questions and have them answer for themselves.
5. Ask Ss some short discussion questions such as...

    -Have you ever been to Southeast Asia?

    -Have you ever gone bungee jumping?

    -What is your favorite TV show? Have long have you been watching it?

Practice More

Part A

1. Ask Ss a warm-up question such as...

    -Have you ever forgotten your umbrella when it was raining?

    -Have you ever stayed up all night?

    -Have you ever skipped English class?

2. Have Ss look at the chart and check Yes or No for the things listed.
3. Have Ss, in pairs, ask each other about the activities.
4. Have Ss ask the follow up questions listed to the right of the activities to the ones their partner said yes to.
5. Ask the class to share any interesting stories their partners told them.

6. Ask a few Ss the questions. Have some of them answer for themselves and some of them answer for their partners.
7. Ask Ss a short discussion question such as...

    -Have you ever told a really big lie?

    -Have you ever forgotten a friend's name?

    -Have you ever eaten really unusual food?

Part B

1. Choose two Ss to demonstrate the dialogue given in front of the class.
2. Have Ss, in pairs, choose one of the activities listed below the dialogue and change the example for that activity.
3. Choose two more Ss to demonstrate a dialogue using one of those activities.
4. Have Ss, in pairs, make dialogues for the all the activities listed.
5. Take a poll of the class to see how many people have done which things.

    For example:

    -Who has played in a band? Who has played the guitar? Who has played the synthesizer?
6. Write the number of Ss on the board next to the activity.
7. Have Ss, in small groups, discuss the results.
8. Write the following questions on the board for discussion:

    -Are you surprised by the results? Why or why not?

    -Which one surprised you the most? Why?

    -Which one were you expecting? Why?

    -Do you think there are lots of different kinds of people in this class?
9. Choose two Ss to read the other example dialogue in front of the class.
10. Have Ss, in different pairs, ask each other about the things listed below, using the dialogue as an example. They should use a few different time formats of the ones given.
11. Ask the class about some of the activities, For example:

    -Who plays the piano? How long have you been playing the piano?

12. Ask Ss a short discussion question such as...

    -Who likes to go jogging?

    -How long have you been jogging?

    -Who has taken an online English course?

    -How long have you been taking an online English course?

    -Who writes a daily journal?

    -How long have you been writing a journal?

Let's do it! 1

Part A

1. Ask Ss a warm-up question such as...

    -Do you like to try new things?

    -Do you like to play sports?

    -Do you like to travel?

    -Are you an adventurous person?

2. Have Ss, individually, check the sports they've played, the foods they've tried, and the places they've traveled to.

3. Have Ss, in pairs, compare the sports they've played.

4. Ask the class about each sport.

    For example:

    -Who has gone horseback riding?

    -What was it like?

    -Who would like to go horseback riding?

5. Have Ss, in pairs, compare the foods they've tried.

6. Ask the class about each food.

    For example:

    -Who has tried Greek food?

    -What was it like?

    -Who would like to try Greek food?

7. Have Ss, in pairs, compare the places they've been.

8. Ask the class about each place.

    For example:

    -Who has gone to Russia?

    -What was it like?

    -Who would like to go to Russia?

9. Ask Ss a short discussion question such as...

    -What is the strangest food you've ever tried?

    -What is the most interesting place you've ever traveled to?

    -What is the most exciting sport you've done?

Part B

1. Have Ss listen to all three of the conversations and fill in the blanks as much as they can.
2. Have Ss listen again to all three and finish filling in the blanks.
3. Check Ss' understanding by asking some yes or no questions such as...

    -Has Michelle gone bungee-jumping?

    -Was Nick scared when he went bungee-jumping?

    -Does Helen want to try Turkish food?

    -Does Ken like Turkish food?

    -Has Bill gone to Bali?

    -Does Megan want a busy, sightseeing vacation?

4. Have Ss listen to the conversations one by one.
5. After each conversation elicit the correct answers to the following questions...

    Conversation 1

    -How many times has Nick been bungee-jumping?

    -Which extreme sports has Michelle tried?

    -Where will Michelle go for bungee-jumping?

    Conversation 2

    -Which foreign foods has Helen tried?

    -What is the most popular, typical Turkish cuisine?

    -What is the Turkish restaurant like that Ken recommends?

Conversation 3

-What are some countries that Megan has visited?

-How does Bill describe Bali?

-Why does Megan want to go to a tropical island?

6. Ask Ss some short discussion questions such as...

-Does anyone here like Turkish food? Why?

-Has anyone been to Bali? What was it like?

-Has anyone been bungee-jumping? Who would like to try it?

Part C

1. Have Ss, individually, think of two things to add to each topic above. (two other extreme sports, two other foreign foods, two other places to travel) and write them underneath the ones already listed.

2. Choose two Ss to read the example dialogue in front of the class.

3. Have Ss, in pairs, discuss their experiences with sports, food and travel. Tell Ss to use the activities listed above as well as their own two additions. Have them use the example dialogue and the listening script on page 108 as an example.

4. Encourage Ss to be creative and ask some detailed questions.

5. Ask for volunteers to share some interesting stories about sports, food, and travel.

6. Ask Ss some short discussion questions such as...

-What sport would you like to try next? Why?

-What food would you like to try next? Why?

-Where would you like to travel next? Why?

Let's do it! 2

Part A

1. Ask Ss a warm-up question such as...

-Do you have long-term hobbies?

-Do you prefer to try a lot of different things or be an expert in one thing?

-How much time do you spend on your hobbies?

2. Have Ss, individually, think of some things they have been doing for a long time.

3. Have them write some long-term activities down. Tell them they can use the examples listed, but they should come up with at least one other thing.
4. Have Ss read the example sentences below.
5. Have Ss write down sentences for each of the activities they have been doing for a long time.
6. Have Ss, in small groups, share at least two of their activities and how long they have been doing them.
7. Ask a few Ss to share a sentence with the class.
8. Ask Ss a short discussion question such as...

   -What is a new thing you have been doing lately?

   -Has anyone had the same hobby for over five years? What have you been doing?

   -What is one hobby that you tried and didn't like?

Part B

1. Have Ss listen to the three conversations.
2. Have Ss listen to all three again and mark true and false for each statement.
3. Elicit the correct answer to each of the statements by asking them in yes or no question form...

   -Has Jennifer been going out with a rock musician?
4. Have Ss listen to the conversations one by one.
5. After each conversation elicit the correct answer to the following questions.

   Conversation 1

   -Who has Jennifer been going out with?

   -How did they meet?

   -What is Jennifer's job?

   Conversation 2

   -What award did Mark get?

   -Why did he get that award?

   -How many times has he gotten the award?

Conversation 3

-Who is interviewing Susan?

-How does Susan look?

-What is her secret to keeping fit and staying young?

6. Ask Ss a short discussion question such as...

    -Have you ever gotten an award? What was it?

    -Have you ever dated someone famous? Who was it?

    -Have you ever been interviewed by someone?

Part C

1. Ask Ss a warm-up question such as...

    -Who is that in the picture?

    -What is he doing?

    -Do you like doing volunteer work?

2. Have Ss, individually, think of one thing they have been doing successfully. Give some examples: volunteer work, sports, competitions, work performance, health, study, etc.

3. Choose 2 Ss to read the example dialogue in front of the class.

4. Have Ss, in pairs, ask about each other's successful thing. Tell them to use the example dialogue.

5. Ask some pairs present their dialogues.

Reading

Part A

1. Ask Ss a warm-up question such as...

    -Have you done any great things in your life?

    -What do you think the first picture is about?

    -What do you think the second picture is about?

2. Have Ss, individually, read the two passages.

3. Have Ss, in pairs, read the passages together. Each student should read one passage.

4. Check Ss' understanding by asking questions such as...

-In the first passage, what places has this person been to?

-What's the best part of this person's travels?

-In the second passage, how many expeditions has Marcus been on?

-What are the good parts of climbing?

-What is one bad part about climbing?

Part B

1. Have Ss, in pairs, discuss questions 1-4.
2. Ask questions 2-4 to the whole class.
3. Ask Ss short discussion questions such as...

    - What is one great thing you've done?

    - Why is it great?

    -How long have you done it?

Writing

1. Have Ss, in small groups, discuss each of the things on the list. Give them the following examples of asking questions about the activities...

    -Have you ever read more than five books in a month?

    -Have you ever taken a cooking class?

    -Have you ever taken a dance class?

    -Have you ever worked as a volunteer?

2. Have the groups choose two of the things on the list that would make their life better. Tell them they are free to write down something not on the list as well.
3. Choose one student to read the example to the class.
4. Have Ss, in class or at home, choose one thing they have tried to do to make their life better and write a similar passage to the example.
5. Choose a few Ss to present their writings to the class.
6. As a class, discuss the writings presented by some of the students.

Unit 6- What's the purpose of your trip?

Get Started

Part A

1. Ask Ss a warm-up question such as...

    -How often do you take trips?

    -Do you like to travel?

    -When was the last time you traveled somewhere?

2. Have Ss, individually, look at the different types of trips and check the ones they would like to take.

3. Have Ss, in pairs, write down some pros and cons to the different types of trips.

4. Have Ss, individually, look at the destinations and check the ones they would like to go to.

5. Have Ss, in pairs, discuss questions 1-3.

6. As a class, discuss the following questions...

    -Who likes to go camping? What are the pros and cons of camping?

    -Who likes to go sightseeing? What are the pros and cons of sightseeing?

    -Who likes to go backpacking? What are the pros and cons of backpacking?

    -Where do you think is the best place to go camping? trekking? sightseeing? shopping? backpacking? to a resort? cruising? skiing?

7. Ask Ss a short discussion question such as...

    -Who has been on a cruise before? Would you recommend it?

    -Who has been to a resort before? Would you recommend it?

    -Who has been to the Mediterranean before? Would you recommend it?

    -Who has been to a tropical island before? Would you recommend it?

Part B

1. Ask Ss a warm-up question such as...

    -Do you enjoy flying?

    -How often do you fly?

    -Do you like staying in hotels?

    -How often do you stay in hotels?

2. Have Ss, individually, match the words to the pictures.
3. Have Ss, in pairs, compare their answers.
4. Elicit the correct word for each picture...

    -What is the word for this picture?

5. Check Ss' understanding by asking some questions such as...

    -Where do you pick up your luggage after the flight?

    -What does a bellhop do?

    -What happens at a security check?

    -What happens at reception?

6. Ask Ss a short discussion question such as...

    -Do you ever have problems when flying?

    -Has anyone ever lost their luggage?

    -What is the most important part of a successful hotel?

Talk Together

1. Ask Ss a warm-up question such as...

    -What do you think the people in the pictures are talking about?

2. Have Ss listen to the dialogue one time with books open.
3. Check Ss' understanding by asking some yes or no questions such as...

    -Is Meg going on a trekking trip?

    -Is Meg going to Nepal by herself?

    -Does Kevin think the trip sounds good?

4. Have Ss, in pairs, read the dialogue, taking turns being Meg and Kevin.
5. Have Ss listen to the dialogue once more with books closed.

6. Elicit the correct answers to the following questions...

    -When is Meg going to Nepal?

    -What will she do in Nepal?

    -What does Kevin think of Meg's trip?

7. Ask Ss a short discussion question such as...

    -Do you have any trips that are lifelong dreams?

-How does Meg's trip sound to you?

-Do you like going on trips by yourself or taking a package tour?

Language Focus

1. Have Ss role-play, in pairs, using the Language Focus example for Reserving a Flight.
2. Have Ss role-play and change the dates and times and places. Give the following example.

    I'd like to make a reservation for one seat to Sydney.

    I want to leave late on Thursday the 12th.

    etc.
3. Ask Ss some questions such as...

    -Is it easy to make reservations for flights here?

    -Do you use the internet, the telephone, or person-to-person communication for reservations?

    -Do you ever buy one-way tickets?
4. Have Ss role-play, in pairs, using the Language Focus example for At immigration.
5. Make sure they use all the different reasons.
6. Ask Ss some questions such as...

    -Is it difficult to go through immigration here?

    -Do you ever get any trouble at immigration?

    -What is the most common purpose for your travel?
7. Have Ss role-play, in pairs, using the Language Focus example for At hotels.
8. Have Ss role-play using the different kinds of hotel rooms for different prices and dates.
9. Ask Ss some questions such as...

    -Are hotels expensive here?

    -Do you enjoy staying in hotels for a long time?

    -What is the best hotel you've stayed in?

Practice More

Part A

1. Ask Ss a warm-up question such as...

    -Where was the last place you traveled by airplane to?

    -What airline was it?

    -How was the flight?

2. Have Ss, in pairs, practice the example given below, taking turns being A and B.

3. Have Ss, in pairs, change the example to fit the information given on the first note.

4. Choose two Ss to demonstrate their dialogue.

5. Have Ss, in pairs, do it for the rest of the notes above. Make sure they know where the times and places should go in the example dialogue.

6. Choose one pair to demonstrate each example.

7. Have Ss make up their own departure, destination, time and date.

8. Have Ss, in pairs, practice the dialogue using their own information.

9. Ask a short discussion question such as...

    -Who has been to Beijing? How was the flight there?

    -Who has been to LA? How was the flight there?

    -Who has been to Florida? How was the flight there?

    -Who has been to Sydney? How was the flight there?

Part B

1. Have Ss, in pairs, practice the example dialogue, taking turns being A and B.

2. Have Ss, in pairs, change the information in the dialogue. Tell them to use the alternate phrases in the box, the Language Focus section, different name of hotels, and different dates and times.

3. Choose a few Ss to demonstrate their dialogue.

4. Ask Ss some discussion questions such as...

    -Have you ever had a bad experience at a hotel?

    -Has a hotel ever lost your reservations?

    -Have you ever tried to travel somewhere and couldn't find a hotel?

Part C

1. Have Ss, in pairs, practice the example dialogue, taking turns being A and B.
2. Have Ss, in pairs, change the information in the dialogue. Tell them to use the alternate phrases in the box, the Language Focus section, different places, different amounts of time, and different attitudes. Tell them that some immigration officers can be quite rude.
3. Choose a few Ss to demonstrate their dialogue.
4. Ask Ss some discussion questions such as...

    -Have you ever had a bad experience at immigration?

    -Have you ever had the wrong visa or papers at immigration?

    -Has your English speaking ever been a problem at immigration?

Let's do it! 1

Part A

1. Ask Ss a warm-up questions such as...

    -How often do you use a hotel's service and facilities?

    -Are hotels in different countries different from the ones here?

    -What's the most common hotel service you use?

2. Have Ss, in pairs, match the pictures with the terms.
3. Elicit a description of each picture. "What service is this picture?"
4. Ask Ss some discussion questions such as...

    -Do you like to order room service?

    -Do you think wake-up calls are helpful?

    -How important is the view from your room?

Part B

1. Have Ss listen to the four phone conversations and fill in the customer's request as much as they can.
2. Have Ss listen to the phone conversations all together and finish filling in the blanks.
3. Check Ss' understanding by asking yes or no questions such as...

-Is there a problem with the temperature in the first conversation?

-Is the person in conversation 2 satisfied with the hotel's services?

-Does the person in conversation 3 order an Asian breakfast?

-Does the person in conversation 4 like their suite?

4. Have Ss listen to the conversations one by one.

5. After each conversation elicit the correct answers to the following questions...

    Conversation 1

    -What room is this person in?

    -What is the problem with their room?

    -What will the hotel do for them?

    Conversation 2

    -What room is this person in?

    -What is their problem?

    -Has it been solved?

    Conversation 3

    -What kind of breakfast does this person order?

    -What comes with an American breakfast?

    -What time will the breakfast be delivered?

    Conversation 4

    -What room is this person in?

    -What is the problem with the room?

    -How will this problem be solved?

6. Ask Ss a short discussion questions such as...

    -Have you ever had a similar problem to this?

    -Are most hotel employees good problem solvers?

    -Which do you think is the worst problem to have?

Part C

1. Have Ss, in pairs, read the example dialogue, taking turns being A and B.
2. Have Ss, in pairs, practice a similar dialogue using the common requests at the top of the page. Tell them to use the listening script on pgs 109-110 for an example.

3. Choose a few Ss to share their dialogue with the class.
4. Ask Ss a short discussion question such as...

    -What kind of view do you prefer?

    -Do you think expensive hotels are worth the money?

    -Do you like organized tours?

Let's do it! 2

Part A

1. Ask Ss a warm-up question such as...

    -Why are tropical islands popular vacation spots?

    -Would you like to live on a tropical island?

    -What are some problems with tropical islands?

2. Have Ss, in pairs, talk about which island they would like to visit the most and why.
3. Ask a few pairs to share what they discussed.
4. Have Ss, individually, check all of the activities they would like to do on their tropical island.
5. Have Ss, in pairs, compare the activities they chose and why.
6. Ask a few pairs to share what they discussed.
7. Separate the Ss into groups depending on which island they want to go to the most.

    For example:

    -Who wants to go to Bali the most? All of you go to this corner of the room...

8. Have the groups discuss why their island would be the best one to visit. Tell them to include the activities from the list that are available for their island.
9. Have the different groups debate each other on why that island is the better choice for a vacation.
10. Ask Ss some discussion questions such as...

    -What is sea walking? Has anyone ever been sea walking?

    -Has anyone ever been white water rafting? Where?

    -Has anyone ever been paragliding? Where?

Part B

1. Ask Ss a short warm-up question such as...

    -Where is the most popular place to go for honeymoons?

    -Why is it the most popular?

    -What kind of place is best for a honeymoon?

2. Have Ss listen to the couple talking about their honeymoon in Bali.

3. Have Ss listen again and fill in their itinerary as much as they can.

4. Check Ss' understanding by asking some yes or no questions such as...

    -Do Julia and Alex both want to go to Bali?

    -Are they going to go scuba diving on the first day?

    -Will they get a massage on the last day?

5. Have Ss listen one more time and finish filling in the itinerary.

6. Elicit the itinerary for each day...

    -What will they do on the first/second/third/fourth/fifth day?

7. Elicit the correct answers to the following questions...

    -Who made all the plans?

    -Does Julia appreciate Alex making the plans?

    -Which day is the busiest?

    -What are the marine sports they will take part in?

8. Ask Ss a short discussion question such as...

    -Does this sound like a good honeymoon to you? Why?

    -Would you like to do scuba diving, sea walking and surfing on the same day?

    -How would you change Alex and Julia's plans for you?

Part C

1. Ask Ss a warm-up question such as...

    -Do you plan every detail of your vacation before you leave?

    -Do you like to be spontaneous?

    -How much time do you usually have for relaxing on vacations?

2. Have Ss, in pairs, read over the itineraries for the trips to Cebu and Fiji.

3. Have each student prepare a description of the itinerary, similar to that in the listening scripts for Part B on page 110. In each pair one student should prepare for Cebu and one for Fiji.

4. Have Ss, in pairs, ask and answer questions about the trips that they planned.

5. Choose a couple of pairs to present their dialogues to the class.

6. Have Ss, in pairs, choose one other tropical island vacation (not Fiji, Cebu, or Bali). Tell them they can use the list from Part A if necessary.

7. Have Ss, in pairs, plan out a week-long itinerary for their vacation, using some of the activities listed in Part A.

8. Choose a few Ss to share their vacation plans with the class.

9. Ask Ss a short discussion question such as...

    -Which vacation seems better: Fiji or Cebu? Why?

    -Which vacation seems more active: Fiji or Cebu? Why?

    -Has anyone ever been to a rainforest? Has anyone ever gone coconut touring?

    -Has anyone ever ridden a banana boat?

Reading

Part A

1. Ask Ss a warm-up question such as...

    -Which of the three pictures look better? Why?

    -Has anyone ever been on safari? How was it?

    -Has anyone ever been on an international ski vacation? How was it?

2. Have Ss, in groups of three, read the three passages. Each student should read one passage.

3. Choose one student to read the Maldives-Beach Paradise passage out loud to the class.

4. Check Ss' understanding by asking some questions such as...

    -What are some things you can do in the Maldives?

    -What is one night activity they recommend in the Maldives?

    -What is one thing you can always find nearby in the Maldives?

5. Choose one student to read the Wild Safari in Southern Africa passage out loud to the class.
6. Check Ss' understanding by asking some questions such as...

   -What are some things to do for adventurous travelers?

   -Where is this safari?

   -What can you see on this safari?
7. Choose one student to read the Snow White Hokkaido passage out loud to the class.
8. Check Ss' understanding by asking some questions such as...

   -What can you do to save money while skiing in Japan?

   -What is a Minshuku?

   -What can you enjoy there?

Part B

1. Have Ss, in small groups, discuss questions 1-4.
2. Take a poll of the class to see where people would like to go out of those three sites.
3. Ask for volunteers to answer the questions in front of the class...

   -Who has a vacation plan in mind? Tell us about it...

   -What is the best tourist site you've visited?
4. As a class, discuss some popular tourist sites in this country.
5. Write some of the tourist sites down.
6. Have Ss, in small groups, rate the sites that you wrote down, picking one site as their favorite.
7. Have each group share their rating and why they chose that site to be their favorite.
8. Ask Ss some short discussion questions such as...

   -What is your idea of a dream vacation?

   -Do you prefer relaxing or being active on vacations?

   -Are you ever nervous or scared about traveling to a new place?

Writing

Part A

1. Ask Ss a warm-up question such as...

    -Do you often write emails when you are traveling?

    -Do you often call home when you are traveling?

    -Do you write a journal when you are traveling?

2. Have Ss read the email from Andy.

3. Check Ss' understanding by asking some questions such as...

    -What are the sights that Andy has seen?

    -What are the sights that he wants to see?

    -How long has he been in London?

4. Have Ss, in class or at home, write an email back to Andy telling him about Korea.

5. Tell Ss to be creative and be sure to include tourist attractions, food and restaurant information, and some comments about Korean culture and people.

6. Ask a few Ss to share their emails with the class.

Unit 7- Could you get me some water?

Get Started

Part A

1. Ask Ss a warm-up questions such as...

    -How often do you request something from someone else?

    -What are some common, everyday requests?

    -What are some requests you make in class?

2. Have Ss, in pairs, match the words with the pictures.

3. Elicit a description of each picture...

    -What is this woman's request about?

    -How does she ask?

    etc.

4. Write some of the phrases on the board...

    -Could you please...

    -Do you mind...

    -Could you...

    -Please...

5. Have Ss, in pairs, try to change the request, using the different phrases. Give the following demonstration if necessary...

    -Could you please answer the phone?-------------Do you mind answering the phone?

6. Have a few Ss share how they changed the request.

7. Ask Ss a discussion question such as...

    -Is it a problem if you are studying and the TV or radio is on?

    -Do you like to drive with the windows rolled down?

    -Do you ever get help from strangers?

Part B

1. Have Ss, in pairs, match the words with the pictures.

2. Have Ss, in different pairs, compare their answers.

3. Choose a few Ss to share their answers.
4. Write the requests on the board and underline why those particular requests are used.
5. Have Ss, in pairs, request things of each other in a similar way. If necessary, write down a few topics on the board...

    -a pencil/pen

    -a piece of paper

    -a book

    -some money

6. Choose some Ss to share their requests with the class.
7. Ask Ss a short discussion question such as...

    -Is smoking allowed many places here?

    -Is it easy to get off early at your work?

    -Are you generous when people want to borrow things?

Talk Together

1. Have Ss listen to the dialogue one time with books open.
2. Check Ss' understanding by asking some yes or no questions such as...

    -Is Kelly having an easy time studying?

    -Does June mind if Kelly borrows his book?

    -Does Kelly get the notes from June right away?

3. Have Ss, in pairs, read the dialogue, taking turns being June and Kelly.
4. Have Ss listen to the dialogue once more with books closed.
5. Elicit the correct answers to the following questions...

    -What exam is Kelly studying for?

    -Where are June's notes?

    -When will Kelly get June's notes?

6. Ask Ss a short discussion question such as...

    -When you were in school, did you borrow notes from your friends?

    -When you were in school, did you lend notes to your friends?

    -Do you like to study in groups or alone?

Language Focus

1. Have Ss, in pairs, ask and answer the questions in the Making Requests section.
2. Ask a few Ss the questions in the Making Requests section and make sure they answer appropriately.
3. Have each student write down three more requests about anything.
4. Have Ss, in pairs, request something from their partner. Their partner should accept or reject the requests.
5. Ask a few Ss for their requests in front of the class.
6. Have Ss, in pairs, ask and answer the questions in the Asking Permission section.
7. Ask a few Ss the questions in the Asking Permission section and make sure they answer appropriately.
8. Have each student write down three more questions of permission about anything.
9. Have Ss, in pairs, ask permission from their partner. Their partner should give or refuse permission.
10. Ask a few Ss for their questions of permission in front of the class.
11. Have Ss get up and walk around the room and make requests and ask permission from their classmates.
12. Ask Ss a short discussion question such as...

    -May I see your homework?

    -Could you tell me your classmate's name?

    -Would you mind switching class times?

Practice More

Part A

1. Have Ss, in pairs, read the example conversation.
2. Explain to Ss that the requests listed on the left should be accepted and the requests listed on the right should be rejected.
3. Have Ss, in pairs, make requests to each other and accept/reject those requests.
4. Choose one pair of Ss to demonstrate each request.

5. Ask Ss a short discussion question such as...

    -Has anyone ever had a cast on their leg? Did you have to ask for a lot of help?

    -Who helps you when you're sick?

    -Do you have many friends that you can ask favors from?

Part B

1. Have Ss, individually, match the two phrases together. Tell them they should be able to tell which one to choose by the language.
2. Have Ss, in pairs, compare their answers.
3. Elicit which phrase goes with which...

    -Which phrase goes with have a dog at home?

4. Have Ss, in pairs, read the conversation below.
5. Have Ss, in pairs ask and answer questions according to the phrases they matched.
6. Ask Ss a short discussion question such as...

    -Are you allowed to have a dog at your apartment?

    -Do you keep your phone on during movies, shows, or meetings?

    -Do you often do people favors?

Let's do it! 1

Part A

1. Ask Ss a warm-up question such as...

    -Do you often ask people for help at work?

    -Do people often ask you for help at work?

    -Do you like working as a team?

2. Have Ss look at the pictures and match the requests to the appropriate people.
3. Make sure they understand that they might have to change the verb tenses to make the requests appropriate.
4. Have Ss, in pairs, compare their answers.
5. Elicit each person's request...

    -What is he/she asking for?

6. Ask Ss a short discussion question such as...

    -Do you ever make copies for people?

    -Do you ever make phone calls for people?

    -Do you ever send packages for people?

Part B

1. Have Ss listen to the four conversations all together.
2. Have Ss listen to all four conversations again and fill in the chart as much as they can.
3. Check Ss' understanding by asking some yes or no questions such as...

    -In conversation 1, did the person get their copies?

    -In conversation 2, did the person get a ride?

    -In conversation 3, did Janet turn her music down?

    -In conversation 4, did Ryan send the fax?
4. Have Ss listen to the conversations one by one and finish filling in the chart.
5. After each conversation, ask the following questions...

    -What was the request?

    -Was it accepted or rejected?

    -Why?
6. Ask Ss a short discussion question such as...

    -Is turning the volume of a radio or TV a reasonable request? Why?

    -Is doing someone's work for them a reasonable request? Why?

    -Is getting someone coffee a reasonable request? Why?

Part C

1. Choose two Ss to read the example dialogue in front of the class.
2. Have Ss, in pairs, make similar dialogues using the expressions in Part A and the Listening Script on page 110.
3. Have each student write down several classroom requests, either to a classmate or a teacher.

4. Have Ss, in pairs, request something from their partner, using the classroom requests they wrote down, the expressions in Part A and the Listening Script from page 110.
5. Ask Ss a short discussion question such as...

   -What are some requests you make from your family?

   -What are some requests you make from your friends?

   -Are there any requests you make from strangers?

Let's do it! 2

Part A

Section 1

1. Have Ss look at the pictures and guess what Peter is asking for.
2. Have Ss listen to Peter asking permission from different people and number the pictures to match the conversations.
3. Elicit a description of each picture...

   -Which conversation is this?

   -What is he asking them for?

Section 2

1. Have Ss listen to all the conversations again and fill in the chart.
2. Check Ss' understanding by asking yes or no questions such as...

   -Does Peter sit down to eat his lunch?

   -Does Peter take the Chemistry 101 class?

   -Does Peter keep the library books?

   -Doe Peter borrow the MP3 player?
3. Have Ss listen to the conversations one by one and finish filling in the chart.
4. After each conversation ask the following questions

   Conversation 1

   -What does Peter ask the stranger?

   -Does the stranger give or refuse him permission to sit down?

   -What was his reason for saying no?

Conversation 2

-What does Peter ask the professor?

-Does the professor give or refuse him permission to take the class?

-What else does the professor say?

Conversation 3

-What does Peter ask the librarian?

-Does the librarian give or refuse him permission to extend the book's due date?

-Why does she refuse?

Conversation 4

-What does Peter ask Tom?

-Does Tom give or refuse him permission to use his MP3 player?

-Why does he refuse?

5. Ask Ss a short discussion question such as...

   -Do you think Peter asks for a lot of things?

   -Do you ask for as many things as Peter?

   -Do younger people ask for permission more than older people?

Part B

1. Choose 2 Ss to read the example dialogue at the bottom of the page.
2. Have Ss, in pairs, ask each other for permission to do the things listed in 1-4. Their partner should either give or refuse permission.
3. Tell Ss to be creative and put some emotion into it.
4. Choose one pair to act out their conversation in front of the class.
5. Ask Ss a short discussion question such as...

   -Have you ever begged for something?

   -Has anyone ever begged you for something?

   -Is it difficult for you to ask for help with things?

Reading

Part A

1. Have Ss look at the magazine article title and guess what it's about.
2. Ask Ss a warm-up question such as...

    -Do you ever complain to anyone?

    -Would you ever write to a magazine to complain?

    -What do you have trouble talking about?

3. Have Ss, in pairs, read the magazine article. Ss should take turns reading.
4. Check Ss' understanding by asking questions such as...

    -How old are the people writing into this magazine?

    -What is the Anna's problem?

    -What is Julie's problem?

Part B

1. Have Ss, in pairs, discuss questions 1-5.
2. Ask the class questions 2 and 3.
3. Ask Ss some more discussion questions such as...

    -What do you think the top problems in your age group are?

    -How do people's problems change when they get older?

    -Do your parents have a problem with anything you do?

    -Do you think its easy to have a roommate?

4. Take a poll and try to find the number 1 complaint in the class.

Writing

Part A

1. Ask Ss a warm-up question such as...

    -Do you think its easier to talk about a problem face to face or on the phone?

    -Do you think its easier to take about a problem on the phone or write a letter?

    -Why do you think writing a letter is much easier?

2. Have Ss, in pairs, read about the situation in the Example and the example letter.

3. Ask Ss some questions...

    -What is the big problem?

    -Would you feel the same way in this situation?

    -Is this a nice letter?

4. Have Ss, in class or at home, write a similar letter using the situation outlined below.

5. Have a few Ss read their letters to the class.

Unit 8- While you are on vacation, what will you do?

Get Started

Part A

1. Ask Ss a warm-up question such as...

    -What do you usually do in your free time?

    -Do you like music?

    -Do you like sports?

2. Have Ss, individually, put the activities they like to do from the list in the correct categories.

3. Have Ss, in pairs, compare their activities.

4. Elicit a description of each of the pictures in the categories.

5. Have Ss, in pairs, ask each other about their free time activities using questions 1-4.

6. Have Ss change pairs and ask their new partner.

7. Ask a few Ss to share one of their partner's free time activities.

8. Ask Ss a short discussion question such as...

    -Who likes to go dancing? Why?

    -Who likes to have parties? Why?

    -Who likes to go trekking? Why?

Part B

1. Have Ss, individually, fill in the chart of what they like to do in specific situations. Tell them they can use the activities from Part A or the ones below.

2. Write on the board...What do you like to do_____?

3. Elicit the question form of each of the specific situations on the chart and write them on the board.

    For example:

    What do you like to do on vacation?

4. Have Ss walk around the room and ask each other different questions from the chart.

5. Point to a student and ask the class...What does he/she like to do on vacation? (for each situation.
6. Ask Ss a short discussion question such as...

    -What do you like to do on rainy days?

    -What do you like to do in the mornings?

    -What do you like to do when you're feeling sad?

Talk Together

1. Ask Ss a warm-up question such as...

    -What do you think these people are talking about?

2. Have Ss listen to the dialogue once with books open.
3. Check Ss' understanding by asking some yes or no questions such as...

    -Does Morris like to go hang-gliding in the winter?

    -Does Olivia want Morris to come to her housewarming party?

    -Did Olivia see a musical last week?

4. Have Ss, in pairs, read the dialogue, taking turns being Morris and Olivia.
5. Have Ss listen to the dialogue once more with books closed.
6. Elicit the correct answers to the following questions...

    -What does Olivia like to do in her free time?

    -What does Morris like to do in his free time?

    -Is Morris going to come to Olivia's housewarming party? Why not?

7. Ask Ss a short discussion question such as...

    -When do you like to go to performances?

    -When do you like to go to parties?

    -Would you like to go hang-gliding?

Language Focus

1. Have Ss, in pairs, ask and answer the example questions in the Time Clauses section.
2. Ask a few Ss the questions in the Time Clauses section and make sure they answer appropriately.

3. Write some other vacation destinations on the board. For example: Kangwon-do, Jeju-do, the mountains, the sea

4. Have Ss apply some of the questions in the Time Clauses section to the other destinations. Their partner should answer appropriately. Demonstrate the following example if necessary.

    -If you go to the mountains, what will you do?

    -I will go trekking and enjoy the fresh air.

5. Ask a few pairs to share their dialogue.

6. Have Ss, in pairs, read the Making Invitations and Accepting/Refusing sections.

7. Ask a few Ss the questions in the Making Invitations section and make sure they answer appropriately.

8. Write a few events on the board such as...study group, dinner party, church, and a date

9. Have Ss, in pairs, invite each other to those other places. Their partner should accept or refuse.

10. Ask Ss a short discussion question such as...

    -After class, what will you do?

    -As soon as you get home tonight, what will you do?

    -Do you accept or reject more invitations?

Practice More

Part A

1. Ask Ss a warm-up question such as...

    -Do you like to be productive in your free time?

    -Do you like to be lazy in your free time?

    -Do you have a lot of free time?

2. Have Ss, individually, fill in the chart for themselves. Tell them they can use the activities listed below, or make up their own.

3. Have Ss, in pairs, ask their partner about their free time activities and fill in the chart for them.

4. Have Ss, in pairs, read the example below.

5. Have Ss, in pairs, interview each other and follow the example below, using the questions at the top and some of the activities listed.
6. Ask a few Ss one of the questions on the chart.
7. Ask Ss a short discussion question such as...

    -Who likes to catch up on sleep?

    -Who likes to go bowling?

    -Who likes to go to exhibitions?

    -Who likes to read comic books?

    -Who likes to travel?

Part B

1. Ask Ss a warm-up question such as...

    -Do you often invite your friends to do things?

    -Do you feel bad if your friends refuse your invitation?

    -Do you ever make up an excuse to refuse an invitation?

2. Have Ss, in pairs, read the example invitation and the example acceptance/refusal.
3. Have Ss, in pairs, invite each other to things and accept or refuse the invitations. Tell Ss to refuse at least half of the invitations.
4. Have Ss walk around the class and invite other classmates. Tell Ss to refuse every invitation and give a reason why.
5. Ask Ss a short discussion question such as...

    -Which is a better excuse, going to a family gathering or finishing reports on the weekend?

    -Which is a better excuse being sick or meeting a friend?

    -Which invitation is the best? Why?

Let's do it! 1

Part A

1. Ask Ss a warm-up question such as...

    -Do you make plans with friends for the future?

    -Do you look forward to events in the future?

    -Do you often get time off of work?

2. Have Ss, individually, make questions using the time adverbs and the phrases given. Make sure they understand that they will have to change some verb tenses.

3. Have Ss, in pairs, ask each other the questions.

4. Have Ss, individually, write down a few more questions using different phrases. For example: After class, As soon as I get paid this month, While I am riding on the subway etc.

5. Have Ss, in pairs, ask and answer each other's questions.

6. Ask Ss a short discussion question such as...

    -After this season is over, what will you do?

    -While you are eating lunch tomorrow, what will you do?

    -Before this week is over, what will you do?

Part B

1. Have Ss listen to all three conversations.

2. Have Ss listen to all three conversations again and fill in the blanks.

3. Check Ss' understanding by asking some yes or no questions such as...

    -Has Cathy decided what to do if she gets a week off?

    -Does Kelly have plans for her trip to Hong Kong?

    -Will Melissa go right home after work?

4. Have Ss listen to the conversations one by one and finish filling in the blanks.

5. After each conversation, ask the following questions...

    Conversation 1

    -What will Cathy do if she gets a week off?

    -What will Denise do if she gets a week off?

    -What would be more challenging-in line skating or scuba diving?

Conversation 2

-What will Kelly do after the semester ends?

-What will she do in Hong Kong?

-What will Amanda do after the semester ends?

Conversation 3

-What will Jim do after work?

-What will Melissa do after work?

-What kind of class does Jim take on Tuesdays and Thursdays?

6. Ask Ss a short discussion question such as...

   -Would you like to take a scuba diving lesson?

   -Would you like to take a dance class?

   -Do you ever visit friends that live in another country?

Part C

1. Choose 2 Ss to read the example dialogue in front of the class.
2. Have Ss think of a few different time situations. If needed, give them the following: If you take a week off, while you are in retirement, When you have a holiday, As soon as you get a free weekend. etc.
3. Have Ss, individually, think of what they will do during these times. Tell them to be creative.
4. Have Ss, in pairs, ask each other about what they will do during these times. Tell them they can use the example and the listening script on pages 111-112.
5. Ask Ss a short discussion question such as...

   -What will you do tomorrow?

   -What will you do this weekend?

   -What will you do if you don't have to work next week?

Let's do it! 2

Part A

1. Ask Ss a warm-up question such as...

    -Where do you find things to do?

    -Do you choose activities where you can meet new people?

    -Do you ever use bulletin boards?

2. Have Ss, in pairs, read the bulletin board activities listed. Each student should read two activities.

3. Have Ss, in pairs, ask each other if tehy would like to do these activities. Tell Ss they should give a reason why or why not.

4. Ask a few Ss if they would like to do those specific activities and why or why not.

5. As a class, take a poll and decide which activity sounds the best and which activity sounds the worst.

6. Ask Ss a short discussion question such as...

    -Has anyone ever been on a cycling tour? Does $100 sound expensive?

    -Has anyone ever gone to a hip-hop show?

    -Has anyone ever taken a magic class?

    -Has anyone ever been to a sculpture exhibition?

Part B

1. Have Ss listen to all four conversations.

2. Have Ss listen to all four conversations again and fill in the blanks in the chart.

3. Check Ss' understanding by asking some yes or no questions such as...

    -Does Gwen want to go to the magic lesson?

    -Will she definitely go?

    -Is Brooke's sculpture going to be displayed in the exhibition?

    -Does she want Eddie to go?

    -Is Jessie excited about the hip-hop performance?

    -Is Jessie a good dancer?

    -Is Amy good at cycling?

    -Does Will try to persuade her?

4. Have Ss listen to the conversations one by one.

5. After each conversation, elicit the correct answers to the following questions...

    Conversation 1

    -How long is the magic show?

    -Is Gwen going to go?

    -Why not?

    Conversation 2

    -Why does Eddie congratulate Brooke?

    -What is her sculpture piece called?

    -When is Eddie going to go?

    Conversation 3

    -How does Derek feel about the hip-hop performance?

    -How does Jessie feel?

    -Are they both going to the hip-hop show?

    Conversation 4

    -When is the cycling tour?

    -How much is the tour? What does that include?

    -Will Amy go? Why not?

6. Ask Ss a short discussion question such as...

    -Who is a good dancer? How often do you do it?

    -Who is a good cyclist? How often do you do it?

    -Who is good at magic? Where did you learn?

    -Who is artistic? What kind of art?

Part C

1. Ask Ss a warm-up question such as...

    -What do you normally do with your friends?

    -What would you like to start doing with your friends?

    -Do you think your friends would like to?

2. Have Ss, in pairs, practice inviting, accepting, and refusing by reading the example dialogue given. They should take turns being A and B.

3. Have Ss, individually write down three activities they normally do with their friends and two activities they'd like to start doing with their friends.

4. Have Ss, in pairs, invite each other to do their activities. They should tell a time and place. Their partner should either accept or politely refuse.

5. Have Ss walk around their room and invite their other classmates to do those activities.

6. Have a few Ss invite the class to do their activities.

7. Ask Ss a short discussion question such as...

    -Do you ever get unusual invitations from people?

    -Do you ever get invitations for dates from people?

    -Do you refuse a lot of invitations?

Reading

Part A

1. Ask Ss a warm-up question such as...

    -Is it easy to take time off from work or school?

    -How often do you take time off from work or school?

    -Would you like to take more time off from work or school?

2. Have Ss, in groups of three, read the three passages about what people do with their time off. Each student should read one passage.

3. Check Ss' understanding by asking yes or no questions such as...

    -Will redflower make definite plans before his trip to Europe?

    -Will gunsnroses be active on his/her time off?

    -Will prettygirl prepare for her holiday?

4. Ask Ss a short discussion question such as...

    -Which of these holidays is the most interesting?

    -Which of these holidays is the most relaxing?

    -Which of these holidays seems like the best experience?

Part B

1. Have Ss, in pairs, discuss questions 1-4.
2. Have a few groups share what they discussed with the class.
3. Ask Ss a short discussion question such as...

    -What is the maximum amount of time you could take off from work or school?

    -When do you think is the best time to take a holiday?

    -Can you take a short time off every year?

Writing

Part A

1. Ask Ss a warm-up question such as...

    -Have you ever traveled to a foreign country?

    -Have you ever backpacked through Europe?

    -Have you ever had any major problems in a foreign country?

2. Have Ss, in pairs, discuss questions 1-3 with each other.
3. Ask a few Ss the questions to see if they answered appropriately.
4. Ask Ss a short discussion question such as...

    -Do you trust people in other countries?

    -Are you careful in other countries?

    -Do you do some research about the countries you are traveling to before you go?

Part B

1. Have Ss, in class or at home, write in detail what they would do in those specific situations.
2. Tell Ss they can use the options listed or their own.
3. Discuss with the class the options listed and if they are good ones...

    -Do you think its a good idea to call the police if you are lost in a city?

    -Do you know how to wire money to people?

    -Could you earn money in a foreign country?

    -Do you think body language is helpful?

4. Ask Ss a short discussion question such as...

   -What will you do if you lose your wallet on your way home?

   -What will you do if it rains this evening?

   -What will you do if you are eating in a restaurant and don't have any money.

Unit 9- What is your ideal type?

Get Started

Part A

1. Ask Ss a warm-up question such as...

    -Is it easy to meet new boyfriends/girlfriends here? Why?

    -How do people normally get together here?

    -How often do you go out on a date?

2. Have Ss, in pairs, look at the comic strip and fill in the blanks.

3. Go around the room and have a student read the next part of the comic strip.

4. Ask Ss a short discussion question such as...

    -Is this the usual process of relationships?

    -What do you think they had in common?

    -Do you often have a crush on someone?

Part B

1. Ask Ss a warm-up question such as...

    -Do you think friendships or romantic relationships are more important?

    -Why do you think so?

    -Do you think people in the same culture have similar ideas about personal relationships?

2. Have Ss, individually, look at the statements and check true or false whether they agree or disagree.

3. Have Ss, in pairs, compare their answers and see if they're the same.

4. Have Ss, in pairs, circle any statements they disagreed on.

5. Go through each pair of Ss and ask them what they disagreed on.

6. Ask each person to defend his/her idea.

7. Take a poll in the class to see how many people agree with which student.

8. Ask Ss a short discussion question such as...

   -What is the best way to break up with someone?

   -Do you believe in love at first sight?

   -Do people ever talk behind your back?

Talk Together

1. Ask Ss a warm-up question such as...

   -Who has gone out on a blind date?

   -How was it? Would you go out on another one?

   -Who hasn't gone out on a blind date?

   -Why haven't you?

2. Have Ss listen to the dialogue once with books open.

3. Check Ss' understanding by asking some yes or no questions such as...

   -Was Kelly satisfied with her blind date?

   -Does Kelly want someone different than her?

   -Will Daniel set Kelly up on another blind date?

4. Have Ss, in pairs, read the dialogue, taking turns being Daniel and Kelly.

5. Have Ss listen to the dialogue once more with books closed.

6. Elicit the correct answers to the following questions...

   -What is Kelly's ideal type?

   -What does she see in the guy she has a crush on?

   -Is Daniel a helpful friend? Why or why not?

7. Ask Ss a short discussion question such as...

   -Do your friends want to set you up on a blind date?

   -Do you ever try to set your friends up on a blind date?

   -Do you feel pressure when you set someone up?

Language Focus

1. Have Ss, in pairs, ask and answer the questions in the Language Focus section.
2. Ask a few Ss the questions in the Language Focus section and have them give the answer in the book.
3. Have Ss, in pairs, ask and answer the questions in the Language Focus section for themselves.
4. Ask a few Ss the questions in the Language Focus section and have them answer for themselves.
5. Ask Ss a short discussion question such as...

    -How many good friends do you have?

    -Do you have a lot more so-so friends that good friends?

    -Have you ever met anyone that is your ideal type?

Practice More

Part A

1. Ask Ss a warm-up question such as...

    -What kind of person are you?

    -What kind of friend do you like?

    -What kind of boyfriend/girlfriend do you like?
2. Choose 2 Ss to read the example dialogue in front of the class.
3. Have Ss, in pairs, make conversations about their best friends using the words in the box. Tell them the first line is for the kind of person they'd like to be friends with, the second line is the name of the person and the third line describes that person.
4. Tell Ss to take turns talking about these friends.
5. Ask Ss, What kind of person would you like to be friends with?
6. Have Ss, individually, pick one of the descriptions given that is best for them. Tell them to write down why it is the best.
7. Have Ss, in pairs, compare their choices.
8. Ask a few Ss to share their and their partner's choices.

9. Ask Ss a short discussion question such as...

   -Which person is the best to be friends with, Tom, Jane, or Ryan?

   -Why do you think that person is the best?

   -Who are you most like, Tom, Jane, or Ryan? Why?

Part B

1. Ask Ss a warm-up question such as...

   -Of the three pictures, which person would you want to be friends with?

   -Why?

2. Choose 2 Ss to read the example dialogue in front of the class.
3. Tell Ss to pretend that they are the people in the pictures.
4. Have Ss, in pairs, interview each other, one partner pretending to be from the questionnaire, and one asking the questions.
5. Make sure Ss take turns being those people.
6. Have Ss, in pairs, ask each other the questions from the questionnaire.
7. Take a poll of the class, asking them the questions from the questionnaire...

   -How many people believe in love at first sight? Why?

   -How many people are dating someone now?

   -What do you like about him/her?

8. Ask Ss a short discussion question such as…

   -What do you look for in a boyfriend/girlfriend?

   -Do you like being single?

   -Are most of your friends in relationships?

|Let's do it! 1|

Part A

1. Ask Ss a warm-up question such as...

   -Are you ever friends with people that you don't really like?

   -Are you very picky about your friendships?

   -Where is a good place to meet new friends?

2. Have Ss, individually, check all the traits that are important to them when making new friends.
3. Have Ss, in pairs, compare their answers.
4. Go through all the traits as a class, ask the following series of questions...

    -What is loyalty?

    -Who thinks loyalty is important?

    -Why is it important?

    -Can you give me an example?

5. Have Ss, individually, circle the traits that are not that important to them.
6. Have Ss, in pairs, compare their answers with their partners.
7. Ask Ss a short discussion question such as...

    -Do you like when your friends make a lot of jokes?

    -Do you like when your friends can listen to your problems?

    -Do you like when your friends can go out and have a great time?

Part B

1. Have Ss listen to all four conversations and fill in the blanks as much as they can.
2. Have Ss listen to all four conversations again and finish filling in the blanks.
3. Check Ss' understanding by asking yes or no questions such as...

    -In the first conversation, does he like a friend who shares his interests?

    -In the second conversation, does she like a friend who cannot keep a secret?

    -In the third conversation, does she like a friend who is selfish?

    -In the fourth conversation, does the person like a friend who is similar to him?

4. Have Ss listen to the conversations one by one and check their answers.
5. After each conversation, elicit the correct answer to the following questions...

    Conversation 1

    -Who is his best friend?

    -What is Ron like?

    -What qualities are important to him?

Conversation 2

-Why is Cathy her best friend?

-What does she think a good friend does?

-What does she tell Cathy?

Conversation 3

-What do her and Anne do together?

-What is Anne like?

-What is her idea of a good friend?

Conversation 4

-How long have he and Ben been friends?

-What is Ben like?

-What is a good friend to him?

6. Ask Ss a short discussion question such as...

-Whose best friend seems like the best? Why?

-Whose idea of a good friend is most similar to yours?

-Is it important for you to have a friend for a long time?

Part C

1. Have Ss, in pairs, read the dialogue, taking turns being A and B.
2. Have Ss, in pairs, talk about what they think a good friend is like using the example dialogue and the listening script on pages 112-113.
3. Ask a few Ss to share their partner's idea of a good friend.
4. Ask a few Ss to share their idea of a good friend.
5. Have Ss, in pairs, talk about their best friend and why they like them.
6. Have Ss, in pairs, talk about what they think a bad friend is like. Tell them to think of some opposite qualities from Part A.
7. Ask a few Ss to share their partner's idea of a bad friend.
8. Ask a few Ss to share their idea of a bad friend.

9. Ask Ss a short discussion question such as...

   -Have you ever had a really bad friend?

   -How long have you known your best friend?

   -Have you ever stopped being friends with someone?

Let's do it! 2

Part A

1. Ask Ss a warm-up question such as...

   -Does everyone have an ideal type?

   -Do you like to date people that are really different from you?

   -Do you like to date lots of different kinds of people?

2. Have Ss listen to three women talking about their ideal types.

3. Have Ss listen again and fill in the blanks as much as possible.

4. Tell them the blanks should go in this order...

   -What kind of person it is.

   -What they believe in

   -Their age preference

5. Check Ss' understanding by asking some yes or no questions such as...

   -Does Jane want a younger man?

   -Is Jane a supportive person?

   -Does Sarah care about a man's job?

   -Does Sarah believe in love at first sight?

   -Does Rachel want a much older man?

   -Is Rachel worried about looks?

6. Have Ss listen to the conversations one by one and check their answers.

7. After each conversation elicit the correct answers to the following questions...

   -What kind of person does she want?

   -What are her beliefs?

   -What is her age preference?

8. Have Ss, individually, read all of the women's profiles and all of the men's profiles.

9. Have Ss, in pairs, match the men and women together based on what they're looking for.
10. Ask for volunteers to explain why they matched each person together.
11. Ask Ss a short discussion question such as...

    -Which match do you think is the best? Why?

    -Who would you date from this list? Why?

    -Do you think matchmaking is a good idea?

Part B

1. Ask Ss a warm-up question such as...

    -What is important to you when looking for a mate?

    -Is age really important?

    -Are looks really important?

2. Have Ss, individually, write down their ideal type.
3. Tell them they can include the same information as the people above or get creative and include different information.
4. Ask Ss a short discussion question such as...

    -Do you think your ideal type really exists?

    -Do you think its bad for people to date people that aren't ideal for them?

    -Are you optimistic about love?

Part C

1. Have Ss, in groups of four, discuss their ideal types.
2. Have Ss choose one person in their group that most closely matches their ideal type.
3. Tell them to discuss why that is their ideal type.
4. Have each pair tell the class about what they are looking for and why.
5. Ask Ss a short discussion question such as...

    -Do you think internet dating is a good idea?

    -What are the dangers of internet dating?

    -Is internet dating or matchmaking different from blind dates?

Reading

Part A

1. Ask Ss a warm-up question such as...

    -Have you ever started a romantic relationship with a friend?

    -Do you think its possible to go from friendship to a romantic relationship?

    -Do you think you can be friends after you date someone?

2. Have Ss, in pairs, read about what people think about friendship and dating.

3. Each student should read two people's opinions.

4. Check Ss' understanding by asking some yes or no questions such as...

    -Is Kristen doubtful about her boyfriend?

    -Is Andy married to a friend?

    -Did Richard have a good experience dating his friend?

    -Did Carrie have problems with her friend that became her boyfriend?

5. Ask Ss a short discussion question such as...

    -Who do you agree with the most? Why?

    -Who do you agree with the least? Why?

    -Have you had personal experiences like these?

Part B

1. Have Ss, in pairs, discuss questions 1-5.

2. Ask each question to the class to see if they agree on the answers.

3. For any disagreements, have a small debate.

4. Ask Ss a short discussion question such as...

    -Do you think personal experience changes your opinions?

    -Have you ever had a personal experience that changed your opinion?

    -Can you give me an example?

Writing

Part A

1. Ask Ss a warm-up question such as...

    -When do you think most people start to have crushes on people?

    -When do you think most people start to have boyfriends/girlfriends?

    -Can you remember your first boyfriend/girlfriend?

2. Choose one student to read the example passage about first love.

3. Have Ss, in class or at home, write about their first love. Tell them they should talk about, when it was, who it was, why they liked him/her, what they did about it, and what happened.

4. Have a few Ss share their first love story with the class.

Unit 10- If you won the lottery, what would you do?

Get Started

Part A

1. Ask Ss a warm-up question such as...

    -What is daydreaming?

    -Do you ever daydream?

    -Are your daydreams realistic?

2. Have Ss, in pairs, complete the sentences below with the phrases in the box.

3. Have Ss, in pairs, match the sentences to the pictures of Sally's daydreams.

4. Check Ss' answers by asking...

    -What would Sally do if she were a famous star?

    -What would Sally do if she were slimmer than she is now?

    -What would Sally do if she won the lottery?

    -What would Sally do if she had a boyfriend?

5. Have Ss, in pairs, ask each other what they would do in that situation. If necessary, write one question on the board so they know the format...

    -What would you do if you won the lottery?

6. Ask a few Ss what they would do in those situations.

7. Ask Ss a short discussion question such as...

    -What would you do if you had to move to another country?

    -What would you do if your best friend had to move to another country?

    -What would you do if you could never eat rice again?

Part B

1. Ask Ss a warm-up question such as...

    -How often do you ask your friends for advice?

    -How often do your friends ask you for advice?

    -Do you think you're good at giving advice?

2. Have Ss, in pairs, complete the sentences with the phrases below to match Ben's specific problems.

3. Have Ss, in pairs, practice asking for and giving advice. One student should be Ben and tell the other student their problems and one student should answer with the advice given.

4. Have Ss, in pairs, practice giving advice. One student should be Ben and tell the other student their problems and the other student should think of their own advice to give Ben.

5. Have Ss switch roles.

6. Ask Ss a short discussion question such as...

    -Has a friend ever asked your advice about losing weight? What did you say?

    -Has a friend ever asked your advice about quitting smoking? What did you say?

    -Has a friend ever asked your advice about English? What did you say?

Talk Together

1. Ask Ss a warm-up question such as...

    -What do you think the two people are talking about in the picture?

2. Have Ss listen to the dialogue with books open.

3. Check Ss' understanding by asking some yes or no questions such as...

    -Does Heather like to gamble?

    -Is Ryan really expecting to win the lottery?

    -Would Ryan buy a lot of books if he won?

4. Have Ss, in pairs, read the dialogue, taking turns being Ryan and Heather.

5. Have Ss listen to the dialogue once more with books closed.

6. Elicit the correct answers to the following questions...

    -How does Heather react to Ryan buying a lottery ticket?

    -What would Ryan do if he won the lottery?

    -What would Heather do if she won the lottery?

    -What are Ryan's chances of winning?

7. Ask Ss a short discussion question such as...

    -What would you do if you won the lottery?

    -Do you ever buy lottery tickets?

    -Do you think gambling is wrong?

Language Focus

1. Explain to Ss that the 2nd conditional is often used for unreal or unlikely situations or for giving advice.
2. Have Ss, in pairs, go over the Unreal Conditional section in the Language Focus.
3. Have Ss ask and answer using the questions and answers provided.
4. Have Ss, in pairs, answer the questions given for themselves. Tell them to take turns asking each other.
5. Ask a few Ss what they would do in the Unreal situations.
6. Have Ss, in pairs, go over the Making Suggestions section in the Language Focus.
7. Have Ss ask and answer using the questions and answers provided.
8. Have Ss, in pairs, come up with some alternative advice.
9. Ask a few Ss to share their alternative advice.
10. Ask Ss a short discussion question such as...

    -If you were me, how would you teach this class?

    -If you woke up tomorrow with perfect English, what would you do?

    -What would you do if you found a lot of money on the street?

Practice More

Part A

1. Ask Ss a warm-up question such as...

    -Do you ever wish your life was different?

    -What do you do to change your life?

    -What kind of situations do you often daydream about?
2. Have Ss, individually, match the wants/wishes on the left with the future plans on the right.
3. Have Ss, in pairs, compare their answers.
4. Have Ss, in pairs, read the example dialogue at the bottom of the page.
5. Have Ss, in pairs, make a similar dialogue for the situations given. Tell them the wishes are on the left and what you would do with them are on the right.

6. Check Ss' understanding by eliciting the correct answers for each situation...

    -What would you do if you had a boyfriend?

    -What would you do if you were smarter?

    -What would he do with his dreams of becoming a doctor?

    -What would she do with a passport?

    -What would he do if he got the right job?

7. Ask Ss a short discussion question such as...

    -What would you do with a promotion?

    -What would you do with a new car?

    -What would you do with gift certificate to your favorite store?

Part B

1. Ask Ss a warm-up question such as...

    -Do you think its ever dangerous to give advice?

    -Do you trust your friend's advice?

    -Do you like to deal with problems by yourself?

2. Have Ss, individually, match the problems with the suggestions.

3. Have Ss, in pairs, compare their answers.

4. Have Ss, in pairs, read the example dialogue.

5. Have Ss, in pairs, make similar dialogues using the problems and suggestions above.

6. Check Ss' answers by asking questions such as...

    -I have no idea what to wear to the prom. What should I wear?

    -My co-worker asked me out on a date. What should I do?

    -I am not ready for the presentation tomorrow. What should I do?

    -My girlfriend was upset with me yesterday. What should I do?

7. Have Ss, in pairs, ask each other about the problems and come up with their own suggestions.

8. Ask one student to share their suggestion for each problem.

9. Ask Ss a short discussion question such as...

   -What would you tell a friend that was unsuccessful in business or school?

   -What would you tell a friend that wasn't getting enough sleep?

   -What would you tell a friend that was sad about a breakup?

Let's do it! 1

Part A

1. Ask Ss a warm-up question such as...

   -Are you good at problem solving?

   -Do you get frustrated at unexpected problems?

   -Do you ever panic about problems or situations?

2. Have Ss, in pairs, discuss each problem and the possible solutions.

3. Write the following questions on the board for them to think about...

   -Why is this a problem?

   -What are the possible solutions?

   -What is the best solution?

4. Ask each pair of Ss about a problem and what they discussed. Have them answer each of the questions on the board.

5. Have Ss, in pairs, read the example dialogue.

6. Have Ss, in pairs, make similar dialogues using the problems and solutions they previously talked about. Tell Ss that each of them should answer all the questions.

7. Choose a few Ss and ask them in front of the class what they would do in those situations. Make sure they explain why they would do it as well.

8. Ask Ss a short discussion question such as...

   -What would you do if you went to a restaurant and didn't have enough money to pay the bill?

   -What would you do if you were pick-pocketed on the street?

   -What would you do if you fell down in a messy puddle on the way to work?

Part B

1. Ask Ss a warm-up question such as...

    -Do you think you are a realistic person?

    -What is the opposite of a realistic person?

    -Are you a dreamer?

2. Have Ss look at the game board. Explain that they should ask their partner if they would do the second thing if they were in the first situation. If the partner says no, they should follow the purple arrow. If the partner says yes, they should follow the pink arrow.

3. Have Ss, in pairs, read the example below. Make sure they understand the form...

    -If you _____, would you_____?

4. Have Ss, in pairs, play the game to find out how realistic they are or how much of a dreamer they are.

5. Ask the class...

    -Who is 100% realistic? 80% realistic? 60% realistic? Do you think that's true?

    -Who is a 100% dreamer? an 80% dreamer? a 60% dreamer? Do you think that's true?

6. Have Ss, individually, think of one example that proves they are realistic or a dreamer.

7. Have Ss, in pairs, share their examples.

8. Have a few Ss share their examples with the class.

9. Ask Ss a short discussion question such as...

    -Is it good to be realistic? Why?

    -Is it good to be a dreamer? Why?

    -Do you think anyone is 100% realistic or a 100% dreamer?

Let's do it! 2

Part A

1. Ask Ss a warm-up question such as...

    -Have you ever been job hunting?

    -Do you think its stressful to look for a job?

    -Do you like doing interviews?

2. Have Ss listen to all four conversations at once.

3. Have Ss listen to all four conversations at once and fill in the chart as much as they can.

4. Check Ss' understanding by asking some yes or no questions such as...

    -In conversation 1, has the person found a job?

    -In conversation 2, is the person nervous about interviewing in English?

    -In conversation 3, will the person take their friend's advice?

    -In conversation 4, did the person make a very good impression?

5. Have Ss listen to the conversations one by one.

6. After each conversation, Elicit the correct answers to the following questions...

    Conversation 1

    -Why is the person discouraged?

    -What advice does she give him?

    -Does he take the advice?

    Conversation 2

    -What kind of interview does the person have?

    -Why is the person nervous?

    -What is the advice given?

    Conversation 3

    -Why does the person congratulate her?

    -What is she worried about?

    -What is the advice given?

Conversation 4

-Why is the person depressed?

-How did he/she act nervous?

-What advice was given?

7. Ask Ss a short discussion question such as…

-Do interviews make you nervous?

-Have you ever had an English interview?

-What do you do when you're nervous?

Part B

Section 1

1. Ask Ss a warm-up question such as…

    -What kind of problems do people have when job hunting?

    -Do you ask friends for advice about jobs?

    -Has anyone ever gone to a job-hunting consultant?

2. Have Ss look at the problems listed on the evaluation sheet.

3. Ask Ss about the problems…

    -Which problem is easily corrected?

    -Why is it a problem to lack self-confidence?

    -Which problem is the worst while job-hunting?

4. Have Ss, individually, write down the problems in the blanks of the chart.

5. Ask Ss a short discussion question such as…

    -Are you a punctual person?

    -Do you prepare for professional situations?

    -Has anyone ever told you that you have a weak voice?

Section 2

1. Ask Ss a warm-up question such as…

    -Would you trust a consultant's advice?

    -Do you find it hard to take criticism?

    -Do you appreciate when people try to help you?

2. Have Ss, individually, write the suggestions given into the chart with the correct problems.

3. Choose one student to read the example advice given in the If statement form.

4. Have Ss, in pairs, give each other advice about the problems listed with the advice in the book.

5. As a class, go through the advice given and ask if anyone has any other suggestions that are different from the ones given.

6. Ask for volunteers to give other advice for the problems listed.

7. As a class, brainstorm other problems people might have while interviewing and suggestions to solve the problems.

8. Ask Ss a short discussion question such as…

    -What would you do if you had a problem with sweating when you're nervous?

    -What would you do if you had a weak resume?

    -What would you do if you didn't know how to answer an interview question?

Reading

Part A

1. Ask Ss a warm-up question such as…

    -Have you ever dreamed of being a millionaire?

    -How could you ever become a millionaire?

    -Is it realistic to think you might be a millionaire one day?

2. Have Ss, in groups of four, read the responses to the question "What would you do if you became a millionaire?" Each student should read one response.

3. Check Ss' understanding by asking the following questions...

   -What would the first person do?

   -Where are some places Crystalclear named?

   -What would the second person do?

   -Why would Etbelly quit his/her job?

   -What would the third person do?

   -How is it different from Etbelly?

   -What would the fourth person do?

   -Where would Lifesaver go?

4. Ask Ss a short discussion question such as...

   -Are any of the responses ridiculous?

   -Are any of the responses strange?

   -Would you quit your job if you became a millionaire?

Part B

1. Have Ss, in small groups, discuss questions 1-4.
2. As a class, talk about whose response is the best and why.
3. Have Ss, individually, answer question four. Tell them they should say at least 3-5 things they would do if they became a millionaire.
4. Have each student tell what they would do with their money.
5. Ask Ss a short discussion question such as...

   -What would you do if someone offered you a new car?

   -What would you do if someone offered you lots of money to move to a foreign country?

   -What would you do if you won a full scholarship to study abroad?

Writing

Part A

1. Ask Ss a warm-up question such as...

   -Do you often think of make-believe situations?

   -Do you know how you would react in all situations?

   -What would you do if you were ten years younger?

2. Choose one student to read the example passage given.

3. Ask for a few volunteers to answer, in detail the question written about.

4. Have Ss, at home or in class, write what they would do in the three situations given.

5. Tell them to be as detailed as possible.

6. Have each student read one of their responses to the class.

Extra: Have each student write down an If statement on a small piece of paper. Tell them to be as creative as possible with their questions. Have Ss each pick an If statement from the pile and go around the room, read the question and answer it.

Unit 11- Could you tell me the way to the bank?

Get Started

Part A

1. Ask Ss a warm-up question such as...

   -Are you good at giving directions?

   -Are you good at understanding directions?

   -Can you use a map well?

2. Have Ss, in pairs, match the pictures with the directional phrases.

3. Check Ss' understanding by asking them what each picture says.

4. If necessary, make some drawings on the board to explain what it means to be opposite, go past, go straight, walk along, and turn left.

5. Ask Ss a short discussion question such as...

   -How do you get around the city?

   -If you drive, do you use a navigational system?

   -If you use public transportation, do you use maps?

Part B

1. Ask Ss a warm-up question such as...

   -Is it easy to find places in this city?

   -Do you like exploring and finding new places?

   -Does it ever make you nervous to be in a new place?

2. Have Ss, individually, fill in the blanks in the sentences, using the map.

3. Have Ss, in pairs, compare their answers.

4. Write some of the phrases that they need to use on the board.

   -next to

   -opposite

   -across from

   -behind

   -in front of

   -go straight

   -turn right/left

5. Have Ss, in pairs, go over their answers again, making sure they used some of the phrases.
6. Elicit the correct answer for each sentence.

    -The bank is _____ (in front of) the police station

    -The supermarket is _____ (opposite, across from) the hotel.

    -The pharmacy is _____ (next to) the shoe store.

    -Excuse me. Is there a movie theatre near here? Yes, there is one _____ (behind) the park.

    -How can I get to the park? Go _____ (straight) and turn _____ (right) at the second corner. It's _____ (opposite, across from) the bank.

7. Elicit another description using the map, give the following demonstration...

    -The park is _____ from the bank, _____ from the library, and _____ the movie theatre.

8. Check Ss' understanding by asking some more directional questions, make sure they answer thoroughly, relating it to the other places around it...

    -Where is the hotel?

    -Where is the library?

    -Where is the shoe store?

    -Where is the pharmacy?

    -Where is the bank?

    -Where is the police station?

    -Where is the movie theatre?

9. Ask Ss a short discussion question such as...

    -Do you like to ask people for directions?

    -Does anyone have a hard time asking people for directions?

    -Do you get nervous asking people in foreign countries for directions?

Talk Together

1. Ask Ss a warm-up question such as...

    -Look at the picture, what do you think is happening?

    -Are police officers friendly here?

    -Have you ever asked people for directions?

2. Have Ss listen to the dialogue once with books open.

3. Check Ss' understanding by asking some yes or no questions such as...

    -Is there an Ace Bank around there?

    -Does the policeman know where the Ace Bank is?

    -Does Lucy have to drive or take the bus to the shopping mall?

4. Have Ss, in pairs, read the dialogue, taking turns being Lucy and the policeman.

5. Have Ss listen to the dialogue once more with books closed.

6. Elicit the correct answers to the following questions...

    -Where are Lucy and the policeman?

    -Where is the shopping mall?

    -How can Lucy get to the shopping mall?

7. Ask Ss a short discussion question such as...

    -Do these directions sound complicated?

    -Could you draw a map of your area for someone?

    -Do you like to walk places?

Language Focus

1. Have Ss, in pairs practice asking and answering questions about locations in the first section.

2. Ask a few Ss the questions and have them answer with the ones given.

3. Have Ss, in pairs, tell their partner about where their bank is.

4. Have Ss, in pairs practice asking for and giving directions in the second section.

5. Ask a few Ss the questions and have them answer with the ones given.

6. Have Ss, in pairs, give directions to the bank from their home to each other.

7. Have Ss, in pairs, practice asking and answering questions about distance.

8. Ask a few Ss the questions and have them answer with the ones given.

9. Have Ss, in pairs, in pairs, tell their partner how far away their bank is from their home.
10. Have Ss, in pairs, practice all of the phrases by telling each other about their neighborhood. Give them the following places and make sure they know to use phrases of locations, directions, and distance.

    -the supermarket

    -the convenience store

    -their favorite neighborhood restaurant

    -their friend's house

Practice More

Part A

1. Ask Ss a warm-up question such as...

   -Where is the Town Hall?

   -Where is the 21st Century Pharmacy?

   -Where is the National Park?

2. Have Ss, in pairs, read the example dialogue, taking turns being A and B.
3. Have Ss, in pairs, change the example dialogue to suit the four places listed.
4. Ask four Ss to tell you the locations of the four different places listed.
5. Ask Ss a short discussion question such as...

   -Does this map seem complicated to you?

   -Which business is the furthest away?

   -Which business is closest?

Part B

1. Ask Ss a warm-up question such as...

   -How do I get to the police station?

   -How do I get to the convenience store?

   -How do I get to the St. Louis Church?

2. Have Ss, in pairs, read the example dialogue, taking turns being A and B.
3. Have Ss, in pairs, change the example dialogue to suit the four places listed.
4. Ask four Ss to tell you how to get to the four different places listed.

5. Ask Ss a short discussion question such as...

    -Have you ever gotten really lost?

    -Is it easier to find your way at night or during the day? Why?

    -Does your neighborhood have everything you need?

Let's do it! 1

Part A

1. Ask Ss a warm-up question such as...

    -Have you ever visited a tourist information center?

    -Do you think tourist information centers are helpful?

    -Are you an expert of things to do and places to go in your city?

2. Have Ss, individually, write down their recommendations for places to go in their city. Tell them to try and think of real places, but they can make some up if they don't know any.

3. Have Ss, in pairs, compare their answers and discuss why those are good places.

4. Ask Ss a short discussion question such as...

    -Do you like giving recommendations?

    -Do you take people's recommendations when traveling to a new city/country?

    -Do you ever buy travel books?

Part B

1. Have Ss listen to all four conversations about places to go.

2. Have Ss listen to all four conversations once again and fill in the chart as much as they can.

3. Check Ss' understanding by asking some yes or no questions such as...

    -Does Jeff know where to get new doorknobs?

    -Does Peter know his way around?

    -Does Judy know where Apple Tree is?

    -Will Emily and Jake go to eat chicken?

4. Have Ss listen to the conversations one by one and finish filling in the chart and write the places on the map.

5. After each conversation elicit the correct answers to the following questions...

   Conversation 1

   -What does Amanda need?

   -Where can she get them?

   -Where is Hardy's located?

   Conversation 2

   -Where does Peter need to go?

   -Does Mayumi know how to get there?

   -Where is the T-Car station?

   Conversation 3

   -Where does Judi need to go?

   -What is she looking for?

   -Where is Apple Tree located?

   Conversation 4

   -Where do Jake and Emily want to go?

   -Why are they going there?

   -Where is the Royal Steakhouse located?

6. If necessary, have Ss listen to all conversations one last time to make sure they filled in the map and chart correctly.

7. Check Ss' answers by asking where things are on the map, tell Ss to give details...

   -Where is Hardy's?

   -Where is City Hall?

   -Where is the T-Car station?

   -Where is the CGB Movie theater?

8. Ask Ss a short discussion question such as...

   -Who do you call when you want a restaurant recommendation?

   -Who do you call when you want to know where to go shopping?

   -Who do you call when you want to know where to get your hair cut?

Part C

1. Have Ss, in pairs, read the dialogue, taking turns being A and B.
2. Have Ss, in pairs, change the dialogue to talk about the places they recommended in Part A.
3. Have Ss, in pairs, ask each other for more recommendations.
4. Have Ss, in different pairs, ask each other about placeson the map in Part B.
5. Have Ss, in pairs, ask each other about places around their city.

Let's do it! 2

Part A

1. Ask Ss a warm-up question such as...

    -Does this map look like a big city or a small city?

    -Does your neighborhood look similar?

2. Have Ss listen to all four conversations.
3. Have Ss listen to all four conversations and fill in the map with the places listed below.
4. Check Ss' understanding by asking yes or no questions such as...

    -Is the Chinese restaurant opposite the Japanese restaurant?

    -Is Jody's hair salon across from the Paradise Shopping Mall?

    -Does Helen need to cross the river to get to the Grand Art Performance Center?

    -Is the dental clinic next to the snack bar?

5. Have Ss, in pairs, compare their maps with each other.
6. Have Ss listen to the conversations one by one.
7. After each conversation elicit the correct answers to the following questions...

    Conversation 1

    -Where are Amber and Peter now?

    -Why is Peter there?

    -Why does Peter need to go to the Chinese restaurant?

    -Where is the Chinese restaurant?

Conversation 2

-Where is Jenna now?

-Why does she need to go to Jody's Hair Salon?

-Where is Jody's Hair Salon?

-How long does it take to get there?

Conversation 3

-Where is Helen now?

-Where is she trying to go?

-Why is she going to the Grand Art Performance Center?

-How will she get there?

Conversation 4

-Where does Sean need to go?

-Why is he going to the dental clinic?

-Where is the dental clinic?

-What is his mom going to do for him to make sure he gets there?

8. Ask Ss a short discussion question such as...

   -Do you have a post office near your home?

   -Do you have a dental clinic near your home?

   -Where is the closest shopping mall to you?

Part B

1. Have Ss, in pairs, read the dialogue.
2. Have Ss, in pairs, ask each other about places on the map and how to get there, using the dialogue for an example.
3. Have Ss change pairs and ask each other about different places and how to get there again.
4. Ask a few Ss how to get somewhere from somewhere else...

   -How do I get to Riverside Park from the Post Office?

   -How do I get from Hollywood Photo Studio to the snack bar?

   -How do I get from the bus stop to the apartment complex?

5. Ask Ss a short discussion question such as...

    -Are you scared to get lost in your city?

    -Is it dangerous for people to not know where they are or where they are going?

    -Can you tell north from south from east to west without a map?

Reading

Part A

1. Ask Ss a warm-up question such as...

    -Do you find it difficult to get around a new place?

    -Do you get a map when you travel?

    -Do you like visiting big tourist attractions?

2. Have Ss, in groups of three, read about the three attractions listed in San Antonio. Each student should read about one attraction.

3. Elicit the correct answers to the following questions...

    -What can you see at the Alamo?

    -How much does it cost to go to the Alamo?

    -What award did the Buckhorn Saloon & Museum win?

    -What can you see at the Buckhorn Saloon & Museum?

    -Where is La Villita located?

    -What can you do at La Villita?

Part B

1. Have Ss, in small groups discuss questions 1-3.

2. Ask each question to the class.

3. Ask Ss a short discussion question such as...

    -Have you ever been to San Antonio?

    -Would you like to visit these attractions?

    -Does San Antonio seem like a good place to visit?

    -Do you think your city has good tourist attractions?

Writing

1. Ask Ss a warm-up question such as...

    -Is price important for you when you're shopping?

    -Do you think things that are low-priced are also low quality?

    -Do you like to buy things that are cheap?

    -Do you like to buy luxury items?

    -How often do you go shopping?

2. Choose one student to read the example paragraph to the class.

3. Have Ss, in class or at home, write a similar paragraph with their favorite places to go shopping. Tell them to be as detailed as possible.

4. Have a few Ss share their writing with the class.

Unit 12- Where do you go to school?

Get Started

Part A

1. Ask Ss a warm-up question such as...

    -Do you like school?

    -Is education important in your country?

    -Do you think the education system is good here?

2. Have Ss, in pairs, put all the subjects on the right into the four categories given.

3. Go through each subject with the class and categorize it, and explain if necessary.

    For example:

    -Which category is Physics in? Science.

    -What is Physics? The science of matter and energy.

    -What do you study in Physics? equations etc.

4. Ask Ss a short discussion question such as...

    -Which subjects did you study in high school?

    -Which subjects did you not study in high school?

    -Which subjects do you wish you had studied more?

5. Have Ss, in pairs, discuss questions 1-3.

6. Have each pair present what they talked about, any disagreements they had etc.

Part B

Section 1

1. Ask Ss a warm-up question such as...

    -Is University study more important than high school study?

    -Is it hard to get into University?

    -Is it hard to graduate from University?

2. Have Ss, in pairs, put the majors into the correct categories.

3. Elicit the correct category for each major listed.

Section 2

1. Have Ss, in pairs, fill in the blanks in the sentence with the correct major.
2. Elicit the description of the other majors that are not mentioned.

    -What is Economics? Literature? International Relations? Chemistry? Geology? Engineering? Political Science? Psychology?

3. Have Ss, in groups, discuss the following questions...

    -What did you study in University?

    -Why did you choose that major?

    -What would you like to study more about?

    -What do you think are popular majors these days? Why?

    -Do you think your University study will be helpful for your future?

4. Ask Ss a short discussion question...

    -Which of these fields interest you?

    -Which of these fields don't interest you?

    -Do you think they are all important fields of study?

Talk Together

1. Ask Ss a warm-up question such as...

    -How old do you think the people in the picture are?

    -What do you think they are talking about?

    -Is the name of a University important to you?

2. Have Ss, with books open, listen to the dialogue.
3. Check Ss' understanding by asking some yes or no questions such as...

    -Was Nick accepted to more than one university?

    -Does Nick need any financial support?

    -Does Nick hate private universities?

4. Have Ss, in pairs, read the dialogue, taking turns being Nick and Sarah.
5. Have Ss listen to the dialogue once more with books closed.

6. Elicit the correct answers to the following questions...

    -Which universities was Nick accepted by?

    -What does he want to study?

    -Why is a private college a better choice for him?

7. Ask Ss a short discussion question such as...

    -What is the difference between college and university?

    -Is the university application process a difficult one here?

    -Do colleges offer a lot of financial support here?

Language Focus

1. Have Ss, in pairs, ask and answer the questions given.
2. Ask a few Ss the questions and make sure they answer with the ones given.
3. Have Ss change the first two questions to past form.
4. Have Ss, in pairs, answer the first two questions in the past form (if they finished school) for themselves.
5. Have Ss change the questions, What do you study? What is your major? Why do you study____? to the past form and ask each other those questions.
6. Ask a few Ss the past questions in front of the class.
7. Ask Ss a short discussion question such as...

    -Are majors important?

    -Do you think its good to pick a major that interests you?

    -Do you think its good to pick a major that will make you a lot of money?

Practice More

Part A

1. Ask Ss a warm-up question such as...

    -How often did/do you and your friends talk about school?

    -Did you meet a lot of friends in your major?

    -Do you like to study in a group?

2. Have Ss, in pairs, read the example dialogue.
3. Have Ss, in pairs, practice the dialogue by changing the majors to the ones in the box.
4. Tell Ss to use different questions (such as the ones in the parentheses).
5. Ask Ss a short discussion question such as...

    -Which majors seem interesting? Why?

    -Do many people have double majors?

    -Do many people have minors?

Part B

1. Ask Ss a warm-up question such as...

    -Was high school a fun time for you?

    -Was/Is college a fun time for you?

    -Which one was more work, college or high school?
2. Have Ss, in pairs, read the dialogue for high school, taking turns being A and B.
3. Have Ss, individually, change the information to apply to them.
4. Tell them to make sure to include their school name, their favorite subject, their least favorite subject and what they enjoyed about high school.
5. Tell them to make sure to use the correct verb tense.
6. Have Ss, in pairs, ask each other about their high school experience.
7. Ask a few Ss about their high school experience.
8. Have Ss, in pairs, read the dialogue for college/university, taking turns being A and B.
9. Have Ss, individually, change the information to apply to them.
10. Tell them to make sure to include the name of their school, their major, why they chose that major, and what they enjoyed about college life.
11. Tell them to make sure to use the correct verb tense.
12. Have Ss, in pairs, ask each other about their college experience.
13. Ask a few Ss about their college experience.

14. Ask a short discussion question such as...

    -Did you like your teachers in high school?

    -Did you like your professors in university?

    -Are you still friends with old classmates?

Part C

1. Ask Ss a warm-up question such as...

    -Do you remember your university application process?

    -What do you have to do to be accepted into university?

    -Did you do well on your university entrance exam?

2. Have Ss, in pairs, read the example dialogue.
3. Have Ss, in pairs, change the dialogue using the phrases below.
4. Have Ss think about their university application process.
5. Have Ss, in pairs, ask each other what it was like.
6. Ask a few Ss to share their experience.
7. Ask Ss a short discussion question such as...

    -Did anyone ever study abroad?

    -Was the application process different or the same?

    -Would anyone like to study abroad?

Let's do it! 1

Part A

1. Ask Ss a warm-up question such as...

    -How do people register for university classes here?

    -Do you think the internet is a good way to register for classes?

    -Do classes get full quickly here?

2. As a class, look at the General Education Requirement Course List for 2007 Spring.
3. Go through the different classes and class times. Give any necessary explanations.

4. Have Ss, individually, fill in their class registration form with their information. Tell them to choose some courses they want to take from the list, but to make sure the times are appropriate too.

5. Have Ss, in pairs, compare their list with each others and note any differences.

6. Ask the class...

    -Who signed up for College Composition? Why?

    -Who signed up for Calculus? Why?

    etc.

7. Ask Ss a short discussion question such as...

    -Who took the most credits?

    -What is the average number of credits most people take?

    -Do you prefer the spring semester or the fall semester?

Part B

1. Ask Ss a warm-up question such as...

    -Did you ever have any difficulty registering for classes?

    -Are professors flexible about registration?

    -Are professors strict about class attendance?

2. Have Ss listen to all three conversations.

3. Have Ss listen to all three conversations again and fill in the chart with True False answers.

4. Check Ss' understanding by asking some yes or no questions such as...

    -Is Melinda going to take Economics 200 this semester?

    -Is this the first time Jin is taking Biochemistry?

    -Has Sue finished all of her general education requirements?

5. Have Ss listen to the conversations one by one and check their answers.

6. After each conversation, elicit the correct answers to the following questions...

    Conversation 1

    -Why did Melinda want to talk to Professor Handon?

    -Why can't Melinda take Economics 200 this semester?

    -What does the professor have to do so Melinda can drop the class?

Conversation 2

-What is Eu-jin taking this summer session?

-What degree is she working on?

-What is Jin taking this summer session?

Conversation 3

-Why does Martin have to take 15 credits this semester?

-What does Martin need to complete his general education requirements?

-How many credits is Sue taking this semester?

7. Ask Ss a short discussion question such as...

-Have you ever been in any of these situations?

-Did you ever fail a class?

-Did you ever drop a class?

Part C

1. Have Ss, in pairs, read the example dialogue.
2. Have Ss, in pairs, make a new dialogue using the information from Part A and their own experience as an example.
3. Have a few Ss share their dialogue in front of the class.
4. Ask Ss a short discussion question such as...

-What's the biggest number of credits you've ever taken? Was it a heavy workload?

-What's the smallest number of credits you've ever taken? Was it easy?

-Which do you prefer, taking a lot of courses every semester and graduating early or taking a smaller amount and graduating late?

Let's do it! 2

Part A

1. Ask Ss a warm-up question such as...

-How many years of school have you done?

-Would you like to go back to school?

-What was your favorite time in school?

2. Have Ss, individually, match the schools with the degrees received.

3. Have Ss, in pairs, compare their answers.

4. As a class, go through each school and degree and make sure everything is clear.

5. Ask Ss a short discussion question such as...

    -Can you give me an example of a vocational school?

    -Can you give me an example of a Master's degree?

    -Can you give me an example of a Bachelor's degree?

Part B

1. Ask Ss a warm-up question such as...

    -Look at the pictures, how old do you think each person is?

    -When you were in high school, did you know what you wanted to study?

    -When you were in university, did you know what you wanted to be?

2. Have Ss listen to all three conversations and fill in the blanks as much as possible.

3. Have Ss listen to all three conversations again and finish filling in the blanks.

4. Check Ss' understanding by asking yes or no questions such as...

    -Does Ryan want to go to university?

    -Does Ashley want to be a stockbroker?

    -Does Mark have a job now?

    -Is Christina satisfied with her major?

    -Is Kelly currently in a community college?

    -Does Jason want to get a bachelor's degree?

5. Have Ss listen to the conversations one by one and check their answers.

6. After each conversation, elicit the correct answers to the following questions...

    Conversation 1

    -What does Ryan want to do after high school graduation?

    -What does he want to study?

    -What does Ashley want to do?

    -What does she want to study?

Conversation 2

-What is Mark doing now?

-What does he want to do in the future?

-What does Christina want to study?

Conversation 3

-What is Jason doing now?

-Why does he want to transfer to a university?

-What is Kelly studying?

-What does she want to do in the future?

7. Ask Ss a short discussion question such as...

-Do you have any future study plans?

-Do you have any future career plans?

-Did anyone ever switch majors?

Part C

1. Have Ss, in pairs, read the example, taking turns being A and B.
2. As a class, go through each of the terms at the bottom of the page.
3. Elicit a description of the phrases and any experiences.

    -What does it mean to take a break from studying?

    -Did anyone ever take a break from studying? Tell us about it.

    etc.
4. Have Ss, in pairs, change the example dialogue and use all the phrases at the bottom of the page. Tell them to be creative.
5. Have Ss, in pairs, change the example dialogue to suit themselves. Tell them to use the phrases below and the listening scripts on page 116.
6. Ask a few Ss about their education experiences.
7. Ask Ss a short discussion question such as...

    -What country has a good education program?

    -Does this country have a good education program?

    -How would you change it?

Reading

Part A

1. Have Ss, in groups of three, read the three passages about education systems. Each student should read one passage.
2. Check Ss' understanding by asking questions such as...

   -What is the education system in America like?

   -What is the education system in China like?

   -What is the education system in Germany like?
3. Ask Ss a short discussion question such as...

   -Would you like to have the teacher decide your future like in Germany?

   -Would you like to have the choice between a private or public school?

   -Do you think its good to have a vast and varied school system?

Part B

1. Have Ss, in pairs, ask and answer questions 1-5. Tell Ss to note anything they disagree on with their partner.
2. Have each pair tell what they disagreed on.
3. As a class, write down the pros and cons of the three examples given.
4. Discuss why they are pros and cons and what could be done to solve them.
5. As a class, write down the pros and cons of their country's education system.
6. Discuss why they are pros and cons and what could be done to solve them.
7. Ask Ss some discussion questions on international study programs....

   -Does your country have exchange programs?

   -Do you think studying abroad is a useful education experience?

   -Where would you like to study abroad?

   -Why would you like to go there?

   -Do you think foreign language education is important at a young age?

   -Do you think your country puts pressure on young children?

Writing

Part A

1. Choose one student to read the example passage in front of the class.
2. Have Ss, in small groups discuss questions 1-4.
3. Tell Ss to go into detail when answering the questions.
4. Have Ss choose one question they had a lot to say about.
5. Have Ss, in class or at home, write a passage answering one of the questions.
6. Have a few Ss share their writing with the class.